Winston Churchill, Franklin Delano Roosevelt, Eleanor Roosevelt, John F. Kennedy, Nehru, Einstein, Helen Keller, William Faulkner, R. Buckminster Fuller . . . these are only a few of the famous personalities the author has known and who live in the pages of this fascinating book.

In his more than forty years of broad-ranging experience, Norman Cousins has been an anti-nuclear activist and founder of SANE, a long-time editor of *Saturday Review*, a personal emissary for Pope John XXIII, and the organizer of special projects for the victims of Hiroshima and the Nazi Holocaust.

His ANATOMY OF AN ILLNESS was a runaway bestseller. In it he told his personal story of how, condemned by doctors to die, he called on his own personal strengths and healed himself from within with the help of laughter, positive thinking and love.

HUMAN OPTIONS continues his triumphant affirmation of the dramatic power of the human spirit.

"Each paragraph is a gem . . . a book to be savored!"
—*KANSAS CITY TIMES*

HUMAN OPTIONS

Norman Cousins

BERKLEY BOOKS, NEW YORK

This Berkley book contains the complete
text of the original hardcover edition.

HUMAN OPTIONS

A Berkley Book / published by arrangement with
W.W. Norton & Company

PRINTING HISTORY
W.W. Norton edition / October 1981
Berkley trade paperback edition / April 1983
Berkley mass market edition / October 1986

ISBN: 0-425-09210-0

A BERKLEY BOOK ® TM 757,375
Berkley Books are published by The Berkley Publishing Group,
200 Madison Avenue, New York, New York 10016.
The name "BERKLEY" and the stylized "B" with design
are trademarks belonging to Berkley Publishing Corporation.
PRINTED IN THE UNITED STATES OF AMERICA

Acknowledgments

THE IDEA FOR THIS BOOK was originally suggested by Frances Cooper Thompson, for many years the archivist of the *Saturday Review*. As long ago as 1965, Mrs. Thompson put together a collection of gleanings from my editorials and articles; since then, from time to time, she has added to that assortment. In the *Saturday Review* for April 15, 1978, Susan Schiefelbein took time out from her duties as senior editor of the *Saturday Review,* to go through hundreds of pieces for the selections that went into the special section of the magazine marking my last issue as editor, and those, in a very real sense, are the precursor of this book. The present volume leans heavily on these two sources, though it embodies a substantial amount of new writing and outside material. In acknowledging my debt to Mrs. Thompson and Miss Schiefelbein, I must emphasize that this book would not have been possible without them.

I also wish to express my appreciation to Dori Lewis for her editorial counsel and guidance over many years; to Emily Suesskind and Mary Swift, of *Saturday Review*'s staff, for their ready and talented assistance with this book and countless other matters; to Dana Little and Deborah Appel, who worked with me at the *Saturday Review* during the 1960s; and to Caroline Blattner, of my staff at UCLA, for her help in the preparation of the manuscript.

Bernice Hall, a lifelong friend whose teaching of art has been an art in itself, made the selection of the photographs and arranged the layout.

In a more general sense, I wish to acknowledge my continuing debt to the people who worked alongside me for many years at the *Saturday Review,* beginning with Amy Loveman, Henry Seidel Canby, William Rose Benét, John Mason Brown, Harrison Smith, and J. R. Cominsky, and extending through to Irving Kolodin, Horace Sutton, Roland Gelatt, Richard L. Tobin, Cleveland Amory, Hallowell Bowser, Katharine Kuh,

ACKNOWLEDGMENTS

Walter Terry, Judith Crist, Goodman Ace, John Ciardi, Nathan Cohn, William D. Patterson, Hollis Alpert, Robert Burghardt, Raymond Walters, Jr., Rochelle Girson, Joseph Luyber, Helene Slaght, Pearl S. Sullivan, Lynn White, Thomas Middleton, John Lear, Albert Rosenfeld, Peter Young. Our development was made possible by the confidence and support of E. DeGolyer, George McGhee, Norton Simon, John F. Wharton, Joseph Iseman, Carl Schaeffer, Leo Nevas, Raymond and Patsy Nasher, Philip Klutznick, Louis Marx, Herbert R. Mayes, and Alexander Hehmeyer. Carll Tucker, my successor as editor of *Saturday Review,* did me the honor of inviting me to continue writing *Saturday Review*'s editorials after I left the staff; that invitation was renewed by Robert Weingarten, present owner of the magazine. My relationship with the readers of the *Saturday Review* has been one of the most rewarding experiences within the reach of a magazine editor. I have described this relationship more fully elsewhere; I need add here only that what the readers brought to the magazine was no less important to the growth of the magazine than what the editors tried to bring to them.

N.C.

FOR BILL HITZIG, *lifelong friend, who has gone more extra miles for more people than even the poets dreamed possible*

Contents

The Plan for This Book

THE OPENING CHAPTER is intended to serve as general background. It is in the form of an essay on one man's learning experiences during most of the twentieth century. The rest of the book is printed in the form of individual paragraphs in order to indicate that they are separate observations written at different times and occasions. Ordinarily, these cullings would be set off from each other by asterisks or other printer's markings, but the effect of such a format can go too far in the direction of disconnection. The design adopted uses extra spacing between the items and small capital letters for the first few words in each paragraph.

I am indebted for the idea of this format to *The Practical Cogitator: The Thinker's Anthology*, a book edited by Charles P. Curtis, Jr. and Ferris Greenslet, first published in 1945. It is a remarkable book, one that gets better with the years.

A note about style: One of the failings of the English language is the absence of a single collective term referring to both men and women. Until very recently, the generic word "man" sufficed as a description for the human species. However, as the result of the long-overdue movement for sexual equality, "man" has come into disfavor. But the attempt to find a substitute term has not been without problems. There is something clanking, inelegant, and contrived about the repetitive use of "he or she" and "him or her" or the variants "she/he" and "him/her." The word "person" can be appropriately used in many cases, but it is not without its limitations, especially in philosophical or anthropological references. For the most part, I have attempted to respect the new custom but I have held to the traditional term when to do otherwise would be clumsy.

HUMAN OPTIONS

Norman Cousins

1

The Twentieth Century as Classroom

OVER A PERIOD OF YEARS, the *Saturday Review* published a series of articles under the title "What I Have Learned." The contributors met the eligibility requirement of being sixty-five or older. Having just reached that chronological plateau, I find myself thinking about my own learning during some forty years of exposure to and involvement in cultural and public affairs.

The basic lessons of that learning experience are recorded in some twelve hundred editorials published from 1940 to 1980, augmented by a large sheaf of personal jottings or, to borrow Dag Hammarskjold's term, "markings." This volume is a distillation of those thoughts and impressions, concerns and preoccupations. In that sense it is an autobiographical notebook or day book, put down in the form of gleanings. But it is not autobiography as the term is generally understood. It does not seek to present a sequential life story. I confess that the thought of attempting a genuine autobiography terrifies me. There comes to mind Vannevar Bush's melancholy description of persons "whose days of vigorous building are done, whose eyes are too dim to see the details of the arch or the needed form of its keystone; but who have built a wall here and there, lived long in the edifice, have learned to love it and have even grasped a suggestion of its ultimate meaning; and who sit in the shade . . ."

An autobiography, moveover, presupposes some degree of control over the materials. How does one control that which can only be perceived by others, which is to say, the larger part? Nietzsche is not in my pantheon of philosophical heroes, but I have always been struck by his definition of man as a "hybrid of plant and ghost." How does one command plants or measure ghosts? One of the most controlled autobiographies in the English language is *The Education of Henry Adams*. It was written in the third person by way of staying in command and looking over his own shoulder. Even this device, however, did not always make for a full and fair view. For Adams's attempt to objectify himself made him subjectively harsh. His five-word verdict on his own life, for example, was that his "theory never affected his practice." It was a verdict, of course, that did not fool his readers or dim the lustre of the book.

An autobiographical notebook, one that assembles the materials that went into my learning adventures, is as close as I dare get to a personal history. What is of greatest consequence in a person's life is not just the nature and extent of his or her experiences but what has been learned from them. The book that had the greatest impact on me as a boy of thirteen was Lincoln Steffens's autobiography, in which every encounter and episode led to reflections by Steffens on their meaning and value.

The raw materials of my own learning have not been meagre. I have had the good fortune to travel around the world a dozen times or more, and to visit all the fifty American states. There were also lessons to be learned from a wide number of people who presided over the history of their times. My main problem was not a shortage of experiences but the speed with which they accumulated over the years. I had the feeling that I had failed to learn the lesson offered by T. S. Eliot in *Ash Wednesday*. "Teach us to sit still," he wrote, echoing Pascal's comment that most of the world's ills were chargeable to the fact that not enough men were attached to their chairs. What Eliot and Pascal bemoaned, of course, was the decline of contemplation. It took a serious illness to get me to put meditation ahead of mobility.

Not that the ability to move swiftly is without certain advantages. The airplane made it possible for me to transport my classroom from place to place. When you are high above the clouds, the feeling of fragmentation that is the lot of the earth dwellers disappears. The mind has a chance to regroup itself for consecutive thought. "The sky," said Emerson, "is the daily bread of the eyes." Nowhere in the world is there grandeur of such dimensions and such proximity. Sometimes, when you fly above a storm, you can see vast cloud masses catching the light of the sun and breaking into colors unknown to the mortals below. The result is a Grand Canyon of hues multiplied by infinity.

These are nourishing distractions and I welcome as many as I can find. Indeed, I have accumulated some four dozen skyscapes in my special memory collection. It is the kind of hobby that goes naturally with a job that has the world for its locale.

Is there any single lesson that comes to the forefront out of these multiple experiences and wanderings? The most important thing I have learned is that one of the prime elements of human uniqueness is the ability to create and exercise new options. The ultimate test of education is whether it makes people comfortable in the presence of options; which is to say, whether it enables them to pursue their possibilities with confidence. Similarly, a society can be judged according to the number and range of options of consequence it makes open to its people. What an individual decides to do with his or her life; the mobility of people and ideas and goods; what a person believes or doesn't believe about the great mysteries of life; how people are to be represented in their individual and collective needs and desires—all these involve the options that otherwise go by the name of natural rights.

The American society was put together by men who were option-seekers and option-makers. They knew that the natural tendency of government is to monopolize options. For options in the hands of the people make officeholders nervous. Government officials want to stay in office as long as possible and to increase their power. The security of those officials is in inverse proportion to the prevalence of options that can be exercised by the people. The tangible expression of the political option is the ability of the people to scrutinize the performance of government and to make effective judgments.

A lesson of hardly less importance I have learned is that human beings, whatever their flaws, are potentially capable of meeting the problems they create. I believe that human capacity is infinite, and that no challenge is beyond human comprehension and reach. The greatest gains are not merely connected to the discovery of nuclear fission or the invention of the means by which humans can be liberated from earth gravity. The greatest gains are related to expanding knowledge about the human brain. "I cannot escape," Harlow Shapley said, "the feeling of a responsibility to glorify the human mind . . . even dream about its ultimate flowering into something far beyond the primitive muscle-guider and sensation-recorder with which we started."

The ability of the brain to perceive itself is its most spectacular achievement. In the very act of comprehending itself, the brain is enhanced and augmented. Knowledge becomes evolution and evolution becomes knowledge. In the past two decades, the concept of the human brain has expanded far beyond that of an organ producing thoughts and memories. Professor Richard Bergland of Harvard has developed the concept of the brain as a gland, by far the most prolific gland in the human body. The full inventory of secretions by the human brain has yet to be completed. So far, however, several hundred such secretions have been identified. The brain produces encephalins and endorphins, which moderate pain and help set a stage for recovery. The brain plays a part in the production of gamma globulin, which is vital for the body's immune system. The brain produces interferon, which acts as a cancer-blocking agent. The vast array of substances produced by the brain are all connected to human development, to the fulfillment of human potentialities, to the maintenance of health, and to the war against disease. What is most significant about this process is that the brain's secretions can be stimulated or diminished by thought and behavior and environment.

New knowledge about the functions of the brain fits in with a shift from the germ theory of disease to the breakdown theory—a breakdown in the body's self-regulatory mechanism. This mechanism is at the core of the immunological system. The question that arises is whether the control mechanism is beyond the reach of the conscious intelligence or whether it operates entirely within the autonomic nervous system. Evidence is now accumulating that the human brain is *not* barred from some measure of control over the autonomic nervous system. It is true that the human brain is not consciously aware of all the processes that go on inside the body—the circulation of the blood, the secretion of enzymes, the production of hormones, the workings of the digestive tract, the way muscles are activated by nerves, and so forth. Yet the fact that we may not have this conscious awareness of our internal functions does not necessarily mean that the brain is barred from any control over them.

It would be possible to quote here from numberless medical papers (and not just from documented accounts of yoga practice) to cite instances in which individuals have been able to direct their bodies in ways generally believed to be beyond the reach of the conscious intelligence. At the School of Medicine of the University of California, Los Angeles, I witnessed a demonstration in which a man punctured his flesh in at least a dozen places and proceeded to control his blood flow. Without use of tourniquets or other devices, and without touching the site of the punctures, he was able to slow the flow to a trickle or stop it altogether. Such a performance is not unknown in Eastern cultures but it was startling, to say the least, to see such a demonstration in an American medical school, with a dozen or more physicians as fascinated observers.

"Biofeedback" is the term used to describe such control. Patients are being taught biofeedback at the Menninger Foundation in Topeka, Kansas, and at other medical centers as a means of relieving their migraine headaches or lowering their blood pressure. The evidence is incontrovertible that chemical changes take place in the body as the result of mental functions or moods. This should not be surprising in view of the experience over the years with placebos. Placebos provide ample proof that expectations can have an effect on body chemistry and on the autonomic nervous system. What is most significant about placebos is not so much the verdict they supply on the efficacy of new drugs as the clear proof that what passes through the mind can produce alterations in the body's chemistry. These facts also indicate that the same pathways and connections that come into play through the use of placebos can be activated without placebos. The main ingredient is the human belief system. Confidence in the ability to mobilize one's resources is a prodigious force in itself.

The next great advance in human evolution may well be represented by the ability of humans, working with a new understanding of brain chemistry, to preside over their own beings. Control or self-regulation is central to the upward thrust of human evolution. Conversely, the greatest dangers to the human race have come about through a failure of control or self-regulation. This applies as much to aggregations of people as it does to individuals. Society is a composite personality—a magnification of all the woes and glories that bedevil or enthrall individual human beings. At a time when evidence is accumulating that world problems are getting out of hand, putting the entire species in jeopardy, it becomes necessary to assemble as much knowledge as possible about the capacity of human beings to control themselves and their society.

The main division in the world today is not between democracy and communism, or between any two sets of political or ideological forces. The main division is philosophical. It cuts across national and ideological boundary lines. It has to do with the way human beings define themselves. Some measure only problems and fail to measure themselves. They position themselves for defeat because they see themselves as a species dependent upon or buffeted by circumstances beyond their control. Any view of human beings as belonging to an immutable species, attempting to function under a fixed ceiling, makes despair inevitable. Progress is possible only when people believe in the possibilities of growth and change. Races or tribes die out not just when they are conquered and suppressed but when they accept their defeated condition, become despairing, and lose their excitement about the future. In a remarkable book titled *Man's Presumptuous Brain,* Dr. A. T. W. Simeons connects the decline of Australia's aboriginals not to any systematic outside oppressive forces but to "a psychosomatic expression of hopelessness—a form of suicide." He cites other peoples—the Papuans and the Muruts of Northern Borneo—as examples of people headed for extinction largely because of self-destructive processes resulting from a collective hopelessness.

But there is a more positive definition of human beings, one which spurns measuring devices and recognizes that what lifts human beings above the forecasts of the computers is the ability to deal with imponderables. The uniqueness of human beings is represented by the capacity to do something for the first time.

The most important single lesson I have learned, therefore, is that human capacity is what it has to be. This does not mean that the prodigious problems involved in operating a world society will automatically find solutions. It simply means that the size and complexity of those problems need not be a cause for despair. If we are defeated it will only be because we became weakened and deflected by feelings of helplessness.

There is no single formula for human survival, but the approach to survival has two main elements. The first is that we ought never to minimize or underestimate the nature of the problems that confront us. The second is that we ought never to minimize or underestimate our ability to deal with them. Human potentiality is the least understood and most squandered resource on earth. So long as human beings are capable of growth—intellectual, spiritual, and philosophical—they have a chance, a very good chance. But potentiality also presupposes control. The ability to do things must be matched by the ability to keep them from becoming a wild spew. The ability to create order is no less important to human survival than the ability to overcome famine or to construct great edifices, to write great books or to compose great symphonies.

In the pages that follow, I try to develop the main themes of this opening chapter, not through extended exposition, but through notes that were put down in response to unfolding history. Borrowing a title from Somerset Maugham, this book is a "summing up" in the form of gleanings of what I have learned in the classroom of the twentieth century. Second only to freedom, learning is the most precious option on earth. It enables us not just to survey experience but to preside over it. It elevates existence, in Whitehead's celebrated phrase, to an "adventure of ideas."

2

Learning as the
Natural Habitat
of Options

CHARLES A. BEARD, an American historian, was once asked by a student if he could sum up in five minutes everything he had learned in a half century of teaching and writing. Professor Beard said he could do better than that; he could sum up everything he had learned in four sentences:

1) The bee that robs the flower also fertilizes it.
2) When it is dark enough you can see the stars.
3) Whom the gods would destroy, they first make mad with power.
4) The mills of the gods grind slowly but they grind exceedingly well.

The student's question and Dr. Beard's reply served as the basis for the *Saturday Review* series "What I Have Learned," referred to in the opening chapter. Generally, the form of the response would be the essay. But sometimes it would take the form of pithy sentences, after the fashion of Dr. Beard. Here are some that stick in the mind:

DR. ALBERT SCHWEITZER, to whom I put the question in 1958 at his jungle hospital in Lambarene, said the one thing he had learned in his life was that he had learned nothing. Then he asked if he could think further on the question. The next morning, he said he thought he had perhaps learned a few things after all. He leaned forward and ticked them off on his fingers:

1) If you have something difficult to do, don't expect people to roll stones out of your way.
2) It is not necessary to go off on a tour of great cathe-

drals in order to find the Deity. Look within. You
have to sit still to do it.

3) Reverence for life is where religion and philosophy
   can meet and where society must try to go.

4) The misery I have seen gives me strength, and faith
   in my fellow man supports my confidence in the
   future.

JAWAHARLAL NEHRU, IN 1959, said he was inclined to agree with
Albert Schweitzer's first response to our question. He said he
believed he had learned very little and doubted that he would
change his mind. More than a year later, however, he said he
found his mind reverting to such speculations. Surely, he told
himself, there was something he had learned worth passing
along. Some things came to mind. He had learned from
Mahatma Gandhi that in undertaking a journey it is important
not to lose sight of one's destination. "There will be many turnings along the way," Gandhi had said. "It will be easy to get lost
on attractive bypaths that lead nowhere. Resist deflections."

Nehru said he had also learned that genuine friendships are
rare; "they must be cherished and nurtured."

Yet another lesson: "People in politics must make known
their gratitude to others for any generosity, however small. But
they make a great mistake if they expect others to make known
any gratitude for generosity to them, however large."

Finally: "The higher the office and the greater the responsibility, the greater the loneliness."

POPE JOHN XXIII said he found the question very amusing. It
made him think of the many mistakes he had made, and some
of them were foolish and made him laugh when they came to
mind. Then he said: "I have learned it is very important to
learn something new each year. This year, I am learning Russian." The year was 1963, only a few months after the Cuban
missile crisis, when he did something a pope is not expected to
do: he sent urgent messages to heads of state. He asked President Kennedy and Prime Minister Nikita Khrushchev to recognize their responsibility was not to their national societies
alone but to the entire human race. In the same way, he said,

he learned that a pope must think about the needs and the spirituality of all people and not just Catholics. Some simple things he said he had also learned. Number one: Never hesitate to hold out your hand; never hesitate to accept the outstretched hand of another. Number two: Each person has something of value to offer; in the process of offering it one raises one's station in the world.

THAT SAME YEAR, Nikita Khrushchev, thinking about my question, looked out the window of his Kremlin office for perhaps three or four minutes, then said: "What I have learned is that there are always new things to be learned. I am not too proud to learn from anyone, even a capitalist." The time was less than two months after the Soviet Union and the United States were poised on the edge of nuclear war.

JOHN F. KENNEDY (APRIL 1963): "I need a lot of time to think about the question. Maybe a year or two. Right now, I like to believe that people can be trusted to make the right choices—given enough time and enough facts. One of the difficulties of being in a position of leadership is that there is seldom enough time, never enough facts."

ROBERT F. KENNEDY: "If I had to pick one thing I think I have learned it is that the greatest privilege anyone with high responsibilities can have is to be able to call on those who really know and whose honesty he respects."

ALBERT EINSTEIN, whose ideas are more fully discussed later in this book, said he felt challenged by Professor Beard's pithy aphorisms. He wanted to submit three items for himself:

1) Pay close attention to the curiosities of a child; this is where the search for knowledge is freshest and most valuable.
2) The advent of nuclear energy has changed everything about the world except our way of looking at it.
3) My ideas caused people to reexamine Newtonian physics. It is inevitable that my own ideas will be reexamined and supplanted. If they are not, there will have been a gross failure somewhere.

JOHN DEWEY: "The purpose of education is to enable a person to come into possession of all his powers."

ONE OF THE MOST QUOTED APHORISMS in literature is Alexander Pope's: "A little learning is a dangerous thing." T. H. Huxley pondered its implications. "Where is the person," he asked, "who has enough of it to be out of danger?"

Learning, in this sense, is not without risk; there is always more to be learned. But it is a glorious risk. The only time the risk becomes fierce and unacceptable is when one seeks to avert it.

SPECULATION LEADS TO LEARNING, just as theory leads to science. "If the world were good for nothing else," said William Hazlitt, "it is a fine subject for speculation." If our venture into space did nothing but to excite our speculations, it would be the most productive mental exercise of which the human mind is capable.

WILLIAM JAMES: "The whole drift of my education goes to persuade me that the world of our present consciousness is only one of many worlds of consciousness that exist."

ANY LIFE WORTH LIVING, said Keats, is a continual allegory—"and very few eyes can see the mystery of that life." But we need not be diminished by mystery. Some things we can see, or attempt to see. We can see that it is not the answers but the mystery that leads us on. We can see large possibilities and purposes and attempt to connect the two. We may not know all there is to know about ourselves and others but we know the meaning of mutual dependence. We need not wait until the nature of evil is fully fathomed before it can be confronted. "I have tried," said St. Augustine, "to locate the source of evil and I have failed."

LEO ROSTEN, who has made a way of life out of pursuing and conveying knowledge, talks about *Tsedakah*, the Hebrew word that combines righteousness, charity, and moral obligation. He quotes Maimonides, the great philosopher, whose "Guide to the Perplexed," published in 1190, anticipated the call to reason that characterized the Enlightenment more than five hundred years later. Maimonides, says Rosten, described two forms of *Tsedakah*. One is to help another to help himself. An even higher form is to help someone anonymously and secretly.

Perhaps there is a third form of *Tsedakah*—to help make people comfortable in expressing their natural goodness. Antisentimentalism rules the roost. But people need to be needed; when they lose their sense of connection they feel walled off, edgy, inconsequential. The psychologists and the psychiatrists know how high the price to be paid is for feelings of guilt and wrongdoing. Perhaps there is an even higher price to be paid for feelings of moral blockage.

DR. BERNARD LOWN, the famed Boston cardiologist, once quoted T. S. Eliot as asking: "Where is the wisdom we lost in knowledge? Where is the knowledge we lost in information?"

The sequence is carried even further in the comment by Samuel Johnson: "Knowledge without integrity is dangerous and dreadful." Or Plato: "Knowledge apart from justice is not knowledge but cunning."

ONE MARK OF GENUINE LEARNING is a person's ability to live comfortably and intelligently with the fact that he can't possibly know everything. He feels no shame about the fact that he may be uninformed about a given subject, for he has substantial access to an answer if he really needs it, and he can evaluate the answer. He won't lose himself in unfamiliar terrain where he may grab at the first intelligible answer and not necessarily the most competent one. He knows what a blind alley looks like, and he doesn't clutter himself with facts beyond his needs.

THERE CAN BE no more important education today than education for personal effectiveness and a sense of connection with big events. A truly educated person is one who has reasonable knowledge, if not command, of his environment, who performs those acts that are relevant to his well-being and the well-being of the people around him, who is able to think about and to anticipate the effects of causes and who can help to control the effects by helping to deal adequately with the causes. However impressive our acquisition of world knowledge, however proficient our ability to marry theory to technique, if we cannot use our thinking ability and our skills to work for a safer and better world, our education is incomplete and we are in trouble.

NO MATTER HOW INTENSIVE or prolonged our formal schooling may be, we are only partly educated if we are unable to think abstractly. The truly educated person knows how to make correlations; he can anticipate the connections between causes and effects; he understands the function of qualifiers; he is not intimidated intellectually by complexity. Finally, he knows that the most vital ingredient in the making of decisions is sequential thought.

IF WE WANT KNOWLEDGE without values, we can find it in almanacs. If we want information without motivation, we can get it in computers.

TO AN AMERICAN, facilities for education have long ceased being a phenomenon. The wonder of it has been completely metabolized, along with newspaper deliveries and running water. To most humans on earth, however, education is the most revolutionary part of a revolutionary age. It represents a flying leap from the tenth to the twentieth century. It is a road map out of feudalism. It is the tangible proof of liberation and the first fruits of freedom. It is a certificate of self-respect. It is a whole host of great expectations. It is what people think about and talk about.

THE GREAT FAILURE OF EDUCATION—not just in the United States but throughout most of the world—is that it has made people tribe-conscious rather than species-conscious. It has put limited identification ahead of ultimate identification. It has attached value to the things man does but not to what man is. Man's institutions are celebrated but not man himself. Man's power is heralded but the preciousness of life is unsung. There are national anthems but no anthems for humanity.

RESPECT FOR THE FRAGILITY and importance of individual life is still the first lesson to be learned.

SELDOM BEFORE has there been such a need for trained, scientific thinking in the attack on problems bearing on human destiny. The finest analysis in the world of a problem may be of little use unless it can be transmitted. And transmission of ideas calls for the organization of logic, set down in sequence, with precision and maximum clarity. If a person wants to exercise influence in the society, a good place to begin is with a proper regard for the techniques of expression. A revolution is long overdue in those rarefied reaches of scholarship which hold scorn and contempt for those wayward colleagues who have a manifest desire to be understood by as many people as possible.

THE SCHOOL should be the main source of strength in a free society. Its job is the highest possible development of the individual in terms of his or her skills, the appreciation of the art of living, the ability to take part in the vital decisions being made by his community and by the nation itself. In short, the school should be the key connecting link between the natural capacity of young people and their actual and potential achievements.

WE IN AMERICA have everything we need except the most important thing of all—time to think and the habit of thought. Thought is the basic energy in human history. Civilization is put together not by machines but by thought. Leadership today requires not so much a determination to outsmart the other fellow as an understanding of the lessons of human experience. It requires a profound knowledge of the diseases of civilizations. It requires ability to anticipate the effects of actions. In short, it requires thought. There is no point in passing the buck or looking for guilty parties. We got where we are because of the busy man in the mirror.

WE HAVE TENDED TO DEBASE the currency of knowledge. We have used terms like egghead or highbrow to beat down any taste or respect for advanced learning. We have almost made thoughtfulness seem like a disfiguration of the human personality. Bookishness has been twisted somehow into freakishness—as though it were possible to build on historical experience without books.

THE PURPOSE OF EDUCATION is to create a higher sense of the possible than would occur naturally to the undifferentiated intelligence. This must mean more than relieving the terror caused by confrontation with the unknown. It must mean developing a zestful capacity for dealing in abstractions and, indeed, for regarding abstractions as the prime terrain for exploration and discovery. Such terrain is filled with what William James called creative "mists and vapors," the vital ingredients of true artistry.

No abstraction, of course, is as potentially hazardous or fruitful as the individual's knowledge of and access to himself. Education's job is to improve this access. The hoped-for effect is the recognition of new options.

SOCRATES HAD NO PARTICULAR LIKING for the term "teacher" when it was applied to himself; he preferred to think of himself as an intellectual midwife. What is most valuable in the Socratic method is the painstaking and systematic development of a thought from its earliest beginnings to its full-bodied state. The mind was fully engaged; this was what was most vital to the process.

CHARLES DARWIN WAS RIDING on a London bus-top when some key thoughts of his theory of evolution burst upon him. This doesn't mean that there is something about the topside of a London omnibus that triggers profound ideas on the origin of the species. What it does mean is that Darwin had allowed his mind to fill up with a complex problem until it spilled over into the subconscious. The result was that, even when he did not consciously direct his thoughts, his mind kept working away at the problem, sorting all the factors that were being accumulated, weighing them, making correlations, and engaging in all the operations leading to a deduction or a discovery. It was the gestative process of ideas, rather than the environment of a bus-top, that was responsible for the flash that electrified Darwin.

H.L.F. HELMHOLTZ, the noted German physicist who died near the turn of the century, described three principal stages in effective thinking. In the first stage, a problem is carefully examined in all its aspects and all directions. In the second stage, ample time is allowed for a problem or an idea to get through to the subconscious in order that the mind may work on it and develop it even when not specifically focused on it. The third stage involves the conditions or circumstances under which an idea is brought to full term and makes its appearance. Helmholtz's analysis may not hold for all people—nothing is more individualistic than a man's thoughts—but at least he emphasizes the need for thought about thinking. Most of our confusion, James Harvey Robinson once wrote, comes from this failure to give thought to thought.

A CASUAL ATTITUDE toward human hurt and pain is the surest sign of educational failure. It is also the beginning of the end of a free society. Long before many children learn to read, they learn how to turn on a television set. They are quickly introduced to a world of howling drunks, pampered idiots, wild-swinging and trigger-happy bullies, and gyp artists. They learn that sex is just another toy, to be discarded when a flashier one comes along. They learn that the way to express disagreement with a man or your distaste for him is to clout him on the jaw or pour hot lead into his belly.

Education is not just what takes place in a building marked "school." Education is the sum total of all the experiences and impressions to which a young and plastic mind is exposed. The parent who insists on sending his child to the finest schools, but who sees no problem in allowing that child to spend at least an equal amount of time looking at TV gangster serials, should not be surprised if the mind of his offspring gives back the meanness and the sordidness put into it.

THOUGHT IS the basic ingredient in learning. It is also the basic energy in human history. Civilization is put together not by machines but by thought. Similarly, human uniqueness is represented not just by our ability to make objects but to sort them out and relate them. Other animals practice communication; only humans have the capacity for comprehension. Displace or eliminate thought, and the species itself has no more claim on survival than the dinosaurs with the four-foot skulls and the pea-sized brains. The impotence of the brute alongside the power of the sage is represented by thought.

WE HAVE MORE FOOD than we can eat. We have more money per person than anywhere else in the world. With six percent of the population we hold eighty percent of the wealth. We have bigger homes, bigger television sets, bigger cars, bigger theaters, bigger schools. We have everything we need, in fact, except the most important thing of all—time to think and the habit of thought.

THERE IS NO OBJECTIVE WAY of determining whether it is good or bad to have increased leisure time during those years when one is not required or even permitted to be part of the accredited community of producers. My guess is that leisure is an option in freedom. There is no impassable distance between the option of freedom and the full exercise of it.

A WHOLE NEW WORLD of potential leisure has sprung up for which people are unprepared. The shorter work week may produce premature retirement symptoms rather than a condition of creative liberation. That is, available new hours are more likely to lead to helplessness and floundering than to active discovery of exciting new options.

Retirement, supposed to be a chance to join the winner's circle, has turned out to be more dangerous than automobiles or LSD. Retirement for many people is literal consignment to no-man's land. It is the chance to do everything that leads to nothing. It is the gleaming brass ring that unhorses the rider.

THE DOMINANT TYPES of boredom in modern civilization, of course, are the result of shorter work weeks, shorter work days, earlier retirement, and increased life expectancy. The causes are surging technology, rodent control, conquest of microbes, muscular unionism, and adroit politics.

WHY SHOULD WE SUPPOSE that inactivity is invariably benevolent? There is the inactivity that restores, of course; but isn't there also the inactivity that destroys through withdrawal and decay? What about the person who doesn't know the difference between relaxation and lifelessness? Obviously, total rest and inactivity may be essential ingredients of relaxation for certain people under certain circumstances at certain times; but it should be equally obvious that immobility is not quite the same as serenity. A state of inaction is not the same as a state of grace.

THE WILL TO LIVE and everything that goes with it are indigenous parts of the liberal arts. It is in this direction that education may find its greatest energy and widest area of service. The relationship between the good life and the good society remains the most insistent item on the joint agenda of education and the nation.

SCHOOLING TENDS TO BE diagrammatic and categorical, opening up no sluices in the human imagination on the wonder and beauty of our unique estate in the cosmos. Little wonder that it becomes so easy for our young to regard human hurt casually or to be unmoved by the mandates of sensitivity.

THE AREA IN WHICH a poor education shows up first is in self-expression, oral or written. It makes little difference how many university courses or degrees a person may own. If he cannot use words to move an idea from one point to another, his education is incomplete. The business of assembling the right words, putting them down in proper sequence, enabling each one to pull its full weight in the conveyance of meaning—these are the essentials. A school is where these essentials would feel at home.

THE FIRST PURPOSE of education is to enable a person to speak up and be understood. Incoherence is no virtue. Feeble language is the surest reflection of a feeble mentality. Even as an affectation rather than a basic condition, stereotyped inarticulateness tends to slow down and cheapen the entire verbal faculty. The trouble with four-letter words and foul language is not so much that they are offensive as that they are weak precisely at the points where they are supposed to be be strong. Through incessant, indiscriminate use, they lose their starch and produce a flabbiness in the total effect. They devitalize everything they touch.

NOT EVERYONE IS LUCKY ENOUGH to be wealthy. But no one need be impoverished in language, nor need anyone be deprived of the distinction that comes from using words with strength and grace. The English language may not be as suitable as the German for scientific purposes, especially in medicine; and it may not have the suppleness and music of French; but in range, depth, and precision it is unsurpassed by any other Western language.

THROUGH THE CENTURIES, the refinement of language has become one of the prime achievements of the human mind, thanks largely to people who regarded the creative use of words as the ultimate art. As a result, English has never been static; it has been constantly tested, refined, and enriched. At times, it has suffered the ordeal of regression. The present age may be one of those bleak periods. This, then, is the time for all lovers of the language to recognize that it is in trouble and to make an effort, a very special effort, to give it the attention it requires.

WALTER LIPPMANN'S *The Good Society* pondered the ability of democratic institutions to grow and respond to the complexities and upheavals of the modern world. In the past half-century, more social and political change has come about than had been experienced in the previous five hundred years. And the most important lesson to be learned from this period is that there is nothing in the nature of a free society that prevents it from rising to all its challenges. Answers take shape out of values. The extent of our commitments to these values, and the urgency we attach to them, will govern the final result. Freedom works best not when it pursues easy goals but when it seeks out ever more difficult ones.

SOCRATES WAS THE MORAL MAN whose hold on history proceeds out of the fact of his death. His death enabled him to become a living symbol of those who fight to defend ideas. The paradox of Socrates, of course, was that the Athenians who opposed him were troubled by what they regarded as Socrates's belief in superstitions. They believed that Socrates disqualified himself as a teacher by talking about "voices" that no one else could hear or about "demons" that no one else could see. It was in the name of rationalism that Socrates was separated from his students. One wonders whether a teacher today who would take advice from inaudible and invisible sources would fare any better than did Socrates.

THE ESSENTIAL LESSON most people still resist, whatever their level of education, is that they are all members of a single species. The species is crowded inside a single life-support system. The need to make the system livable has yet to dominate human concerns or the intellectual processes.

EDUCATION—the good education, that is—can help us to move out beyond the narrow and calcifying confines of the ego so that we can identify ourselves sympathetically—no, that word is not strong enough—identify ourselves *compassionately* with the mainstream of humanity.

THE HIGHEST EXPRESSION of civilization is not its art but the supreme tenderness that people are strong enough to feel and show toward one another. Art proceeds out of an exquisite awareness of life. The creative spirit and the compassionate spirit are not things apart but kindred manifestations of response to life. If our civilization is breaking down, as it appears to be, it is not because we lack the brainpower to meet its demands but because our feelings are being dulled.

What our society needs is a massive and pervasive experience in resensitization. The first aim of education should not be to prepare young people for careers but to enable them to develop respect for life. Related lessons would be concerned with the reality of human sensitivity and the need to make it ever finer and more responsive; the naturalness of loving and the circumstances that enhance it or enfeeble it; the right to privacy as an essential condition of life; and the need to avoid the callousness that leads to brutalization. Finally, there is the need to endow government with the kind of sensitivity that makes life and all its wondrous possibilities government's most insistent concern.

WE ARE MORE than the shadow of our substance, more than a self-contained and self-sealing entity. We come to life in others and are affected by their hurts or their needs or their moral splendor. When we deny this, we hammer at the essence of our own being.

COMPASSION IS NOT QUANTITATIVE. Certainly it is true that behind every human being who cries out for help there may be a million or more equally entitled to attention. But this is the poorest of all reasons for not helping the person whose cries you hear. Where, then, does one begin or stop? How to choose? How to determine which one of a million sounds surrounding you is more deserving than the rest? Do not concern yourself in such speculations. You will never know; you will never need to know. Reach out and take hold of the one who happens to be nearest. If you are never able to help or save another, at least you will have saved one. To help put meaning into a single life may not produce universal regeneration, but it happens to represent the basic form of energy in a society. It also is the test of individual responsibility.

TOO OFTEN it doesn't enter our minds to consider what Asian and African peoples must inevitably think, given so many decades of experience with white foreigners who assigned them an inferior role and then educated them to accept that inferiority. The idea that the life of a man with yellow or brown skin is worth as much as the life of a white man was not one of the articles of faith brought by the white man to Asia and Africa. It was something the Asians and Africans had to learn by themselves, and it is now going into the greatest revolutionary upheaval in the history of the entire world. We will make no contact with reality in Asia and Africa until we have a searing awareness that nothing that happens in those lands happens as of today; everything that happens is connected to a scarred history.

WE CAN ACCEPT IT AS A FACT that all men are capable of feeling pain and bereavement, that no one is bruise-proof, and that the most fundamental form of persuasion is not political or ideological but moral. The failure to accord the individual human being full dignity is the calamitous failure. Conversely, the acceptance of that dignity is the precondition for any discourse or exchange. This is the primitive and ultimate test of our policy, in Asia or anywhere else. It is also the first evidence of maturity and achievement.

EDUCATION PREPARES US SUPERBLY for a bird's-eye view of the world; it teaches us how to recognize easily and instantly the things that differentiate one place or one people from another. But our education sometimes fails to teach us that the principal significance of such differences is that they are largely without significance. We fail to grasp the fact that beyond the differences are realities scarcely comprehended because of their shattering simplicity. And the simplest reality of all is that the human community is one—greater than any of its parts, greater than the separateness imposed by actions, greater than the divergent faiths and allegiances or the depth and color of varying cultures.

AN ICE AGE can come about inside human beings through a lowering of the temperature of human response. Against this, there is always the possibility that we see our commitment to one another as the basic energy and power of our civilization.

HUMAN BEINGS MUST BE JUDGED by the challenges they define for themselves. So far, they have attached more importance to the challenge of adventure than to the challenge of compassion, more importance to the challenge of technological grandeur than the challenge of human growth, more importance to the challenge of war than the challenge of peace, more importance to the challenge of productivity than the challenge of perspective, more importance to the challenge of the scientific intelligence than the human spirit.

YOUNG PEOPLE TODAY want a larger share in the decision-making about their lives. However much respect they may have for the superior learning of their teachers, they believe they themselves have something of value to offer in the determination of what it is they should be taught and even how they are to be taught. They see themselves not just as receptacles for instruction but as essential participants in the educational experience. They mirror the central tendency of the age—which is the quest for individual respect. Finally, they shun those for whom thinking is reflexive, rather than reflective, and increasingly subject to computerized decisions.

YOUNG PEOPLE TODAY tend to be tough-minded but they are also tenderhearted. They cannot be pushed around—intellectually, socially, or politically. They can smell humbug or hypocrisy a mile away. They can't be fobbed off with slick formulations, and they don't lend themselves to manipulation—whether by government, teachers, parents, or even their own peers. They place proper value on human feelings as well as on human needs. They will literally turn the world upside down to combat cruelty or injustice. They have no particular fondness for organizations as such, but they like to work closely together so long as things don't become too formal or institutionalized. Above all, they shun artificiality and ostentation. They see no reason for disguising or changing the natural look of things. They are perhaps more a puzzlement to their parents than they would have been to their great-grandmothers, who baked their own bread, knitted socks and sweaters, loved folk songs, and thought that fancy makeup actually detracted from the good looks of young girls. They are not afraid to go all the way in behalf of a moral or spiritual conviction and are literally determined to bet their lives on what they consider to be a moral principle. They have no difficulty in recognizing the dominant challenge of the time, which is to comprehend the meaning of human oneness as well as to be able to accept allegiance to the family of man. They know that war, in the context of weapons of absolute destruction, has become total insanity, and they are unimpressed with the tradition that says there is no other way.

WE HAVE EVOLVED in every respect except in our ability to protect ourselves against human intelligence. Our knowledge is vast but does not embrace the workings of peace. Because we attach importance to a rounded view of life we study history, philosophy, religions, languages, literature, art, architecture, political science. Because we are concerned about our well-being we study anthropology, biology, medicine, psychology, sanitation. Because we are interested in technical progress we study chemistry, physics, engineering, and mathematics. But we have yet to make the making of peace central to our education. The basic principles involved in creating a situation of safety on earth are left to random speculation. Yet unless these principles are understood and applied, nothing else we know will do any good.

Santayana: "We must welcome the future remembering that soon it will be the past. And we must respect the past, remembering that once it was all that was humanly possible." One might also say that all that is humanly possible stretches before us, made possible by the mistakes of the past.

KNOWING MORE about the gift of life is not merely a way of satisfying random curiosity. In the end, it is what education is all about.

"IDEAS," says W. Macneile Dixon, the English philosopher, in his *The Human Situation,* "are the most mysterious things in a mysterious world. . . . They are beyond prediction. They appear to have a life of their own, independent of space and time, and to come and go at their own pleasure. . . . They are living, powerful entities of some kind, and as infective as fevers. Some, like flowers, are the creatures of an hour; others are of a prodigious vitality and root themselves, like oaks, in the soil of human nature for a thousand years. Ideas, like individuals, live and die. They flourish, according to their nature, in one soil or climate, and droop in another. They are the vegetation of the mental world."

JAMES RUSSELL LOWELL viewed ideas as the ovarian eggs of the next generation's or century's civilization. "These eggs are not ready to be laid in the form of books as yet," he wrote, "some of them are hardly ready to be put into the form of talk. But as rudimentary ideas or tendencies, there they are and they will go into the making of the future."

THE PAST sets up far fewer barriers to the understanding of causes and effects than does the present. You assemble your reference materials about the past; there they rest, accessible and obedient, waiting to be sorted out and judged. But the facts of the present won't sit still for a portrait; they are constantly vibrating, full of clutter and confusion.

Today's elusive and complicated facts, however, are apt to be viewed as simplicities a generation hence. And all the current sophistications will probably seem like a species of innocence. What happens, of course, is that people never lose their innocence; they just take on new perspectives. This is where nostalgia begins. It is also what makes the reading of history so engaging and the writing of it so precarious.

NOTHING IS EASIER than to denounce the evildoer; nothing is more difficult than to understand him. So wrote Dostoevski out of his preoccupation with the incestuous relationship between good and evil. William James pondered the same phenomenon and concluded that different persons have different thresholds of crossover from good to evil; no one can anticipate the circumstances under which his own crossover might occur.

ALMOST A CENTURY before Toynbee offered his challenge-and-response theory of history, Ludwig Gumplowicz, an Austrian philosopher, wrote that "out of friction and struggles, out of separations and unions of opposing elements, finally come forth . . . the higher cultural forms, the new civilizations, and the new unities."

New unities are now in the making. Whether they come in time will depend not on historical or anthropological laws but on the confidence human beings have in their ability to transcend old limitations. If this is what the new probings on the next development of mankind are all about, then we may be on the verge of the most exciting period in history.

THE AMERICAN PEOPLE may have lost their natural abundance, but they need not have lost their natural sense of adventure. The grand leaps of the creative intelligence and the resolute determination that pushed back the American frontier can now be put to work on the most magnificent research project of all time—creating a human habitat congenial not just to the human physical presence but also to the human spirit.

NOTES ON C.P. SNOW's "Two Cultures": The main problems of the two cultures is not an absence of communication but the nature of what is being communicated. The artist and the scientists are talking to each other but not about the right things. They are not applying their creative brainpower and advanced skills to the largest need of the species of which they are both a part. Each culture serves its own traditions without addressing itself to the problem of a world that has become one before it has become a whole. The need today is for a third culture—one concerned with the total connection between total cause and total effect, one which recognizes that tribalism and human safety don't mix.

THE ULTIMATE DIVISIONS take place within societies, not between them. On one side are those who perceive that new connections among men have to be created regardless of their diversity and who move almost instinctively toward building those universal institutions that can serve the city of man. On the other side are those who think in terms of separatism, perpetuation of group egos, the manning of tribal battle-stations, and the benefits of compartmentalization. It is out of this transcendent confrontation that "Everyman" will make his voice and weight felt. He needs to be encouraged to believe that what he feels and wants to say can be part of a universal thrust.

THE DETHRONING OF DOGMA, apparent in politics and ideology, has not spared education and philosophy. New and open currents are at work everywhere. People are breaking through traditions and barriers that obstruct or run counter to ideas of human unity. The familiar notion that a meeting of East and West can best be brought about by a confluence of Eastern spirituality and Western technology is now giving way to the perception that the greatest differences are not between cultures but within them.

CONSIDER THE PROVINCIALISM of philosophers and scholars who place peoples and civilizations in two big bundles marked "East" and "West." We may live in the two worlds of "East" and "West" but we have only one planet to do it in. The designations "East" and "West," applied to religion and philosophy, are relics of an outmoded scholarship. There is too much variety within Europe and the Americas, on one hand, and Asia and Africa on the other, to warrant the use of these terms in any but a purely geographical sense.

THE LANDS AND CULTURES of humankind today are various, but they are all compressed into a single geographic abode. The question to be determined in our time is whether this abode can be preserved for human life or whether it will become the arena of the last great combat. The means are now sufficient to punish nature itself, to put a torch to all our works, and to deprive us of the decencies that have given us distinction and pride.

WHAT IS THIS CRISIS COMPLEX that opens our eyes to our mutualities only when raw disaster seems but inches away, and then just as promptly closes them to anything but differences as soon as those inches become yards? The tendency seems rooted in human nature but that is no reason to preserve it, intensify it, and exploit it.

ONE OF THE GREAT PARADOXES in history is that the truest expression of Christianity is to be found not in the West but in the East. In India countless millions of people are living out the ideas of Christ, though they do not call themselves Christians and are unfamiliar with Christian theology. They are the poor, the meek, the merciful, and the pure in heart. They regard life as sacred and will not harm it in any of its forms. They practice renunciation. They believe in nonviolence and they worship the memory of a human being who perhaps has come closer to enacting Christianity than anyone in modern history. Interestingly enough, Gandhi's struggle was directed against a Western Christian nation.

WE MAY NOT BE ABLE to persuade Hindus that Jesus and not Vishnu should govern their spiritual horizon, nor Moslems that Lord Buddha is at ' : center of their spiritual universe, nor Hebrews that Mohammed is the major prophet, nor Christians that Shinto best expresses their spiritual concerns, to say nothing of the fact that we may not be able to get Christians to agree among themselves about their relationship to God. But all will agree on the proposition that they possess profound spiritual resources. If, in addition, we can get them to accept the further proposition that whatever form the Deity may have in their own individual theology, the Deity is not only external but internal and acts through them and that they themselves give proof or disproof of the Deity in what they do and think; if this further proposition can be accepted, then we come that much closer to a truly religious situation on earth.

TO THE EXTENT that any religion speaks only in behalf of its own interests, to the extent that it places itself above or apart from the whole, it jeopardizes its own interests and injures the whole. In order to get inside man, the Church must get outside itself.

LET THE GREAT RELIGIONS cease explaining their differences to each other and begin to chart the elements of basic unity that could serve as the building blocks for common action. If religions are the custodians of the spirit of man, and if that spirit is imperiled, then responsible action is possible and essential.

ALL THE WORLD's great spiritual leaders have derived their power largely by making the supreme identification; namely, by offering their lives in the cause of human need or ennoblement. Each of these leaders was aware that the example of renunciation and sacrifice awakens powerful forces in human beings.

NEVER BEFORE have there been so many churches and temples; never before has the institution of man been in greater jeopardy. Christianity has not truly involved itself in the human situation. It has become strangely adjacent to the crisis of man, seemingly content with trying to create a moral and spiritual atmosphere instead of becoming a towering and dominant force in the shaping of a world congenial to man. It has become one of the values we fight for instead of a force in itself. It is not regarded as the working source of wisdom and strength for conscience. It has yet to become supremely pertinent and supremely effective in safeguarding the commonwealth of man at a time of peril so profound as to be incomprehensible to the rational intelligence alone.

WHAT IS AT STAKE TODAY is not primarily Christian civilization or Jewish civilization or Islamic civilization or Hindu civilization or any other. To the extent that any religion speaks only in behalf of its own interests, to the extent that it places itself above or apart from the whole, it jeopardizes its own interests and injures the whole. In order to get inside man, the Church must get outside itself.

IN AN AGE of saturating frustration, the lot of the theologians is perhaps the uneasiest of all, for they are trying to give life not merely to religious doctrine but to the moral imagination. They are trying to impart substance, reality, and relevance to religious ideas, but their words are absorbed as tentative sound without changing the color or the shape of the walls of the mind. The churchmen realize this and struggle all the harder to create human adequacy for human crisis. But to do that it is necessary first to decompartmentalize man, to enable him to move easily and naturally from theology to action—action that is morally effective and effectively moral. And this is not a simple thing to do, even for the men of God.

IT SHOULD NOT BE DIFFICULT for the individual to determine what the great spiritual leaders in history would say in the present situation. They would say that it is not enough for man to profess oneness with other men; we must act it out. It is not enough to wear the garment of religious identification; we must accept its ethical and moral obligations and glory. It is not enough to lay claim to personal sacredness; we must bind ourselves to it through respect for it and sensitivity to it. It is not enough to boast of the gift of a rational intelligence; we must nurture it, work it, apply it, defend it. It is not enough to prate about justice; we must create a basis for it in the world itself.

THERE HAS NOT BEEN a great ideal or idea which has not been perverted or exploited at one time or another by those who were looking for the means to an end—the end being seldom compatible with the idea itself. The greatest idea ever to be taken up by the mind of man—Christianity—was for centuries violated and corrupted by its very administrators. Alexander's vision of a brotherhood of man fell victim to its own force—the force which based right upon might.

Mohammed dreamed of a universal religion based on the noblest of ethics and taught that conversion by the sword was no conversion at all, yet his followers built an empire largely at the point of a sword. That is the double nature of the challenge: To bring about world community and to keep it pure. It is a large order, perhaps the largest order human beings have had to meet in their fifty-odd thousand years on earth, but they have set up the conditions which have made it necessary.

THE HUMAN SPECIES is the term that describes the complex, contradictory, unpredictable two-legged animal that has, at one and the same time, limitless potentialities for good and for harm but who, unless it is careful to avoid artificial and absurd distinctions based on the shape of his skull or the pigmentation of skin or the name of the church or the name of a father, may within a short time find itself part of a universal fury of self-obliteration.

IT IS NO ACCIDENT that the Declaration of Independence begins with a reference to a "decent respect to the opinions of mankind." These words do not mean that all that is required is an awareness of the existence of other people. What they mean, if anything at all, is that the rights and welfare of other people are no less important than our own.

THE AMERICAN PEOPLE see a reflection of their own early history in those peoples who do not yet own their own nations. They see the cause of freedom from outside rule as a cause that connects all men. They accept that connection and are inspired by it.

IN LOOKING BACK AT their own past, and in assessing their purposes and ideals, the American people also look to the duty that unites them to all mankind—to create an enduring peace under law for this generation and the generations to come; to make the world safe for its diversity; to advance the cause of independence wherever peoples are not free and to create a pattern of interdependence for the whole; to use the resources of nature and the intelligence of man in the common good; to serve man's capacity to be free; and to justify the fact of life. This is the ideology. It is real and it is ours.

THERE ARE NO "MERE" MEN. Moral splendor comes with the gift of life. Each person has within him a vast potentiality for identification, dedication, sacrifice, and mutuality. Each person has unlimited strength to feel human oneness and act upon it. The tragedy of life is not in the fact of death but in what dies inside us while we live.

NO ONE NEED FEAR DEATH. We need fear only that we may die without having known our greatest power—the power of our free will to give our life for others. If something comes to life in others because of us, then we have made an approach to immortality.

NO PERSON can be truly at peace with himself if he does not live up to his moral capacity.

IT IS THIS that we all share—the emergence of a common destiny and the beginning of a perception, however misty, that something beyond the nation will have to be brought into being if the human race is to have any meaning.

3

Survival as
an Option

THE HUMAN SPECIES is unique because it alone can create, recognize, and exercise options. This means it can do things for the first time. We can reasonably argue, therefore, that human beings are equal to their needs, that a problem can be resolved if it can be perceived, that progress is what is left over after the seemingly impossible has been retired, and that the crisis today in human affairs is represented not by the absence of human capacity, but by the failure to recognize that the capacity exists.

IS IT POSSIBLE to be an optimist in a world which has turned most of its organized brain power and energy into the systematic means for debasing life or mutilating it or scorching it or obliterating it? What basis is there for hope when the human future is increasingly in the hands of men who do not comprehend the meaning of the new power and who are, some of them, puny and fretful and prone to act out of frustration or false pride or mistaken notions of grandeur?

CAN ANYONE BELIEVE in the ability of the human species to eliminate the mass injustice that leads to mass violence—or the mass violence that feeds back into mass injustice? Can anyone have confidence in the capacity of human intelligence to sustain the natural environment on which humans are absolutely dependent—at a time when the progressive despoliation and poisoning of air, land, and water are fast outrunning efforts to protect the environment?

QUESTIONS LIKE THESE are producing a profound upheaval within the body of contemporary Western social philosophy. For the essence of modern social thought is its belief in the idea of human progress. With a few exceptions, such as Spengler, the leading thinkers of the past few centuries have generally accepted Aquinas's idea that man "advances gradually from the imperfect to the perfect." Pascal underscored this notion when he said that man is a creature capable not only of undergoing experiences but of comprehending them, and that the unending accumulation of experiences is therefore bound to be reflected in his own learning, understanding, and growth. Bacon, Descartes, Kant, and Hegel, each in his own way, have attempted to break free from the medieval concept of fixed limitations on human potentiality, or the Lucretian idea of cataclysmic disaster, or the prophetic notion of doom.

NO GROUP OF THINKERS has had more to say about the potentialities of human beings, especially under conditions of freedom, than Americans such as Franklin, Jefferson, Emerson, William James, Holmes, Pierce, and Dewey. Each has added depth and strength to the idea that humankind is capable of almost infinite development. Indeed, emerging from the ideas of the American social philosophers is a definition of human uniqueness: the ability to do that which has never been done before.

Today, however, the bedrock of modern social philosophy has been badly shaken by a long series of somber developments pointing toward the ultimate dismemberment of human society. The habit of violence is no less significant than the technology of violence. There has been a growing desensitization to human hurt.

HISTORY IS AN ACCUMULATION of causes and effects, but it is far from being a procession of inevitables. Time and again supposedly inexorable forces have been reversed by human acts proceeding out of positive human decisions. To say that human beings are locked into error and delusion runs counter to human experience. This is not to underestimate our propensity for error. But neither should we underestimate our ability, through an act of will, to create a wide and exciting range of new possibilities. The only ultimate prison we need fear is our inertia and indecision.

THE ANSWER, THEN, is that it *is* possible to be an optimist in today's world—without having to strain or synthesize. It is necessary only to attach oneself confidently to a plan for accomplishing an essential purpose and then help bring that plan to life with advocacy and work.

OPTIMISM SUPPLIES the basic energy of civilization. Optimism doesn't wait on facts. It deals with prospects. Pessimism is a waste of time.

NOTHING IS EASIER than to turn cynical; nothing is more essential than to avoid it. For the ultimate penalty of cynicism is not that the individual will come to distrust others but that he will come to distrust himself. It is not necessary, in order to avoid cynicism, to believe blindly that human beings are always good. It is necessary only to scrutinize history. What we find is not just a flawed procession but the pursuit of better conditions and even an occasional splash of grandeur. So long as this is so, there is firm ground for believing that the affirmative interludes can be lengthened and perhaps even become dominant. We are required not to invent good human beings but to help give them faith in themselves and to help keep them going.

CYNICISM IS INTELLECTUAL TREASON. If we fail or fall back, it will be because too many men turned sour and because they scorned their own possibilities. The job before us today is not to scoff but to prod. Those of our intellectuals who moan the most about the disappearance of high ideals are providing us with a confession of their own critical shortages. A person with a real ideal has no time for despair.

PROGRESS BEGINS with the idea that progress is possible. Cynicism begins with the notion that retreat and defeat are inevitable.

THE MAIN CHARACTERISTIC of pessimism, like cynicism, is that it sets the stage for its own omens. It shuns prospects in the act of denying them. It narrows the field of vision, obscuring the relationship between the necessary and the possible. "I hate cynicism," said Robert Louis Stevenson, "a great deal more than I do the devil, unless perhaps the two are the same thing."

Pessimism fails because no one really knows enough to be a pessimist. Imponderables are constantly being converted into positive forces under pressure from powerful ideas. The reason there is no inconsistency between the exercise of reason and the optimistic outlook is that the search for new approaches or answers often has to be built on new grounds. Pessimism is a poor range-finder for locating such grounds.

SO LONG AS we do not persuade ourselves that we are creatures of failure; so long as we have a vision of life as it ought to be; so long as we comprehend the full meaning and power of the unfettered mind—so long as this is so, we can look at the world and beyond, to the universe, with the sense that we can be unafraid of our fellow humans and face choices not with dread but with great expectations.

THE ONLY SAFE ASSUMPTION for human beings is that the world will be what we make it. Within broad margins, the movement of history will continue to be connected to human desires. Our dreams and not our predictions are the great energizers. Those dreams may seem at times to be murky and beyond realization. But dreams must command the respect of historians. Dreams put human beings in motion. If the dreams are good enough, they can overcome happenstance and paradox; and the end product will be far more solid than the practical designs of men with no poetry in their souls.

THE BASIC ENERGY of a people comes from their creative capabilities, from their ideas, from their trust in one another, and from their confidence in the integrity of the species. We can learn that a good life is possible without extravagance, and that our obligations are not just to ourselves but to all earth dwellers—and especially to those who have yet to be born. The race is not to the swift but to the sensible.

SOME PEOPLE SAY that human beings cannot possibly develop the comprehension necessary to deal with change in the modern world. But there is a larger view of man, one that history is prepared to endorse. This view holds that the great responses already exist inside man and that they need only to be invoked to become manifest. For humans are infinitely malleable, infinitely perfectible, infinitely capacious. It is the privilege of anyone in a position of leadership to appeal to those towering possibilities.

INEVITABLY, AN INDIVIDUAL is measured by his or her largest concerns. If he is troubled only by what happens to him here and now, then his measurement is quickly taken but it is not necessary to use the long rule. But if a person places a high value on life, whatever its accent or station; if he respects a mysterious but real connection between himself and the people who have gone before him and those not yet born, then there are proportions in his measure beyond estimate. In such a man, perceptions are keenest when he looks inward and sees others in himself. He will fix his mind on the things that are more important to him than whether he lives or dies. The ultimate question for him has to do not with his personal immortality but with the immortality of values and meaningful life beyond his own time.

NOTHING IS MORE IRRESPONSIBLE than to accept the infallibility of the computer. The computer can't be programmed to comprehend the mysteries of human response. The computer has no way of anticipating the advent of a Thomas Jefferson or a Winston Churchill or anyone capable of generating ideas that can lead to great change. Can the computer tell us anything about a mind like Bucky Fuller's—a mind that can conceive of new sources of energy, new ways of building homes and cities, new ways of making the earth more livable?

IT IS PRECISELY because the experts confine themselves to projections based on facts that their predictions are vulnerable. For history is shaped as much by imponderables as by hard facts. The biggest changes of the twentieth century were not foreseen by the experts. They had no way of anticipating the tides of political change that were to sweep over the world. They had no way of knowing where or how human hopes or fears would be suddenly created into vast surges of energy that would transform political, economic, and social institutions.

WE CAN REJECT the notion that the human race is locked into a grim inevitability. No one, no matter how great his or her expertise, knows enough about the future to say that we have passed the point of no return. He may be the supreme authority on his own subject, but he cannot predict the workings of the human mind. The way the human mind will respond to any given situation is the kind of intangible that can become the dominant reality of tomorrow.

ALL THINGS ARE POSSIBLE once enough human beings realize that the whole of the human future is at stake.

THE BIGGEST TASK of humanity in the next fifty years will be to prove the experts wrong.

THE MOST IMPORTANT FACTOR in the complex equation of the future is the way the human mind responds to crisis. In *A Study of History* Arnold Toynbee points out that the greatest historical forces are set in motion when people decide to pit themselves against serious challenge. Human experience is not a closed circle. It is full of magnificent detours and sudden departures from predicted destinations.

THE STARTING POINT for a better world is the belief that it is possible. Civilization begins in the imagination. The wild dream is the first step to reality. It is the direction-finder by which people locate higher goals and discern their highest selves.

LET US THINK ABOUT ourselves. If our purposes are frail, if the value we attach to the idea of progress is small, if our concern for the next generation is uninspired, then we can bow low before the difficulty, stay as we are, and accept the consequences of drift. But if we have some feeling for the gift of life and the uniqueness of life, if we have confidence in freedom, growth, and the miracle of vital change, then difficulty loses its power to intimidate.

IDEALS DO NOT become translated into working reality just because they are needed. They have to ignite in men's minds. They have to develop explosive force. They have to blast their way through mountains of resistance, tradition, and orthodoxy.

WE ARE LEFT with a crisis in decision. The main test before us involves our *ability* to change. That we are capable of change is certain, for there is no more mutable or adaptable animal in the world.

AN IDEA does not have to find its mark in the minds of large numbers of people in order to create an incentive for change. Ideas have a life of their own. They can be nourished and brought to active growth by a small number of sensitive vital minds which somehow respond to the needs of a total organism, however diffused its parts.

THE DIFFERENCE between a statesman and a demagogue is that the statesman is willing to incur serious personal political losses in the pursuit of objectives that may not be achieved in his own lifetime.

NATURE HAS NOT BEEN equally lavish with her endowments, but each person has a certain potentiality in achivments and service. The awareness of that potentiality is the discovery of purpose; the fulfillment of that potentiality is the discovery of strength.

PROGRESS IS what is left over after we meet a seemingly impossible problem.

OVER THE CENTURIES scientists and philosophers have been able to stand on common ground because of a question containing only five words: What is a human being? The more this question is probed, the greater the respect and awe they have for the upward possibilities of human evolution.

WE CREATE IDEALS in the face of a common danger, but we haven't kept them alive in the face of a common hope. The crisis passes but the real trouble begins. It happened to Saul and David when faced with the Philistines. It happened to the Greeks who found an ideal when faced with the Persians, but who lost it after the enemy was beaten. It happened to Rome, which died not because it had been beaten or overthrown but because it had nothing it wanted to live for. It happened only yesterday, in the last war, and there is the threat it may happen again today. There will always be mistakes, contradictions, untold mass suffering, anguish. These are inevitable considering the scope and the nature of the struggle: To fail to look past these dark by-products into the larger needs and the larger ideals is to pass up the greatest opportunity for constructive thinking in history.

PEOPLE ARE UNDERGOING a vast experience in demystification. Old ideas of separatism and group identity don't move them as much as new perceptions of human solidarity. What is happening is that the human race dares to think that ethics can be applied to the behavior of nations and that a time may be approaching when men will not be ordered to kill or be killed. All sorts of magnificent notions are at large in the human mind today, and the most revolutionary notion of all is that the problem of human survival is not beyond human intelligence.

WHATEVER OUR LIMITATIONS, however great our perpetuation of error, what has to be done today is well within our capacity. For what is needed are not superhuman attributes. We are not being called upon to rearrange the planets in the sky or to alter the composition of the sun. We are called upon to make decisions affecting our own welfare. The only price we have to pay for survival is decision.

LOUIS BRANDEIS, one of America's great jurists and thinkers, once said there could be no true community "save that built upon the personal acquaintance of each with each." This observation was perhaps anticipated in Aristotle's comment that in order for a state to function properly, all its citizens should be within the range of a single man's voice. By that definition alone, the entire world has now become a single community. The challenge as far ahead as anyone can see is to give substance to that concept.

NOTHING CAN BE MORE DANGEROUS to a nation than the feeling by any considerable portion of its people that they cannot change the course of history. This feeling leads to indifference. This indifference is not a narrow affair or a sometime thing. It affects the tone and quality of the entire community. It helps to determine a nation's goals and its ability to meet them. It colors the entire range of a nation's sensitivities and its perceptions.

THE BASIC TEST of a society is represented not by what the society does for its people or even by what the people do for the society but by the ability of both the society and its people to comprehend the principles of human perfectability and human growth. These are not marginal principles. They are the principles that make other principles possible.

WE MAY SING the same songs the world over and adopt the same fashions; now let us connect our voices to the concept that our world must be governed.

A MISCONCEPTION is haunting the world. It is the idea that the main danger of war today is represented by the differences dividing the nations. These differences are serious enough, but they are not nearly so dangerous as what the nations have in common. The nations have the same volatile rules in dealing with one another. They put their narrow interests ahead of the common good. They ask for more than they are prepared to give. They will accept no limitations on what they consider to be their right to make unilateral decisions. Codes of morality laboriously built up over the centuries for moderating and governing the behavior of individuals are set aside at precisely the point where they are most needed—the point of confrontation between nations.

War is the price paid by nations for the exemptions they grant themselves—exemptions from objective reasoning and humility. That is why wars grind on to exhaustion: Total subjectivity destroys alternatives and options more thoroughly than bombs destroy cities and villages.

ALL THE WORLD'S institutions of learning, no matter how hallowed and ivied, remain monuments to the collective ignorance of man in the techniques for maintaining and nurturing civilization itself. All the efforts of religions to make men aware of their spiritual resources are largely wasted and marginal unless they have some bearing on the ideas and actions of the national societies in their intercourse with one another. And all the turnings and churnings of men and groups inside the nations—the quest for individual growth and gain, the thrust for even-higher levels of prosperity—all these can only be regarded as distractions so long as the world lacks a rational or workable method for preserving peace.

NO SOCIETY IS SMALLER than the one that sees no obligation to later generations. A society earns its place in history by respecting the unclamorous claims of the unborn.

SOCIETY DOES NOT EXIST APART from the individual. It transfers its apprehensions or its hopes, its fatigue or its vitality, its ennui or its dreams, its sickness or its spirituality, to the people who are part of it. Can the individual be expected to retain the purity of his responses, particularly a sensitivity to the fragility of life, when society itself seems to measure its worth in terms of its ability to create and possess instruments of violence that could expunge civilization as easily as it once took to destroy a village? Does it have no effect on an individual to live in an age that has already known two world wars; that has seen hundreds of cities ripped apart by dynamite tumbling down from the heavens; that has witnessed whole nations stolen or destroyed; that has seen millions of people exterminated in gas chambers or other mass means; that has seen governments compete with one another to make weapons which, even in the testing, have put death in the air?

ONE OF THE PRINCIPAL PROBLEMS in the modern world is that we have delegated our survival instinct to the state. We have become increasingly incapable of comprehending fundamental threats to the species of which we are a part. We have no difficulty in discerning threats to the nation—the nation sees to it that we are fully alerted and mobilized—but we have hardly any response to the fact of overriding danger to life as a whole.

PRIMITIVE MAN had at least one important advantage over modern man. His response mechanism to surrounding dangers was superbly developed and in excellent working order. He may not have been capable of writing lyric poetry or of calculating a price-earnings ratio, but one thing he most certainly could do: He could sense and define a danger before it became full-blown. He didn't waste any time between the initial awareness of the danger and the response.

THE NOTION OF INDIVIDUAL HELPLESSNESS is unhistoric and unnatural. It is a notion that has gained currency at certain times, of which the present is an example. What generally happens is that supposedly inexorable forces gather strength in combination with personalized malevolence. At such times, enough evil is inflicted on enough people to produce a lowering ceiling over human hopes.

THE INDIVIDUAL has a tendency to imitate the state. He cannot be expected to stand totally free of the one institution that overshadows all others. Even when he seeks to resist the violence and irrationality of the state, he tends to speak the language of the state and to adopt its own temper.

THE INDIVIDUAL is the ultimate cause but that cause is defeated if the individual proclaims it for himself. It is the difference between saying "I am as good as you are" and "You are as good as I am." The former statement leads to a breakdown of affirmative and social values. The latter statement prepares the ground for towers of purpose and achievement.

INDIVIDUALITY IS THE ESSENCE of human existence. But this doesn't change the fact that human life has common sources and is confronted by common problems and common needs. Nor does it alter the ultimate question of human destiny—a destiny in which men can retain individuality and yet be held together.

HUMAN BEINGS AND THEIR SOCIETY are in a constant condition of interaction. At a time when nations can vaporize civilization, we take on the temper of the total organism of which we are a part. We reflect an environment that no longer fully comprehends the fragility and uniqueness of human life.

THE MOST SIGNIFICANT PART of the philosophy of the Constitution-makers was the proposition that a good society makes good people. If human beings are in a condition of perpetual and precarious balance between good and evil, the obligation of the good society is to try to keep the scales from being tipped the wrong way.

HOPE IS A GIFT and hope is magic, but hope cannot exist, either in the individual or society, without the prospect of regeneration.

THE CASE FOR HOPE has never rested on provable facts or rational assessment. Hope by its very nature is independent of the apparatus of logic. What gives hope its power is not the accumulation of demonstrable facts, but the release of human energies generated by the longing for something better. The capacity for hope is the most significant fact in life. It provides human beings with a sense of destination and the energy to get started. It enlarges sensitivities. It gives values to feelings as well as to facts.

AMERICANS ARE BEING UNDERUSED and their full potentiality is not being developed if they are poorly educated, poorly fed, poorly sheltered. The management of natural resources begins with the management of human resources.

THERE IS PRIMITIVE, colossal energy in the simply stated but insistent call by enough people for a situation of reasonable safety on earth, for an end to anarchy in the dealings among states, and for easier access by members of the human family to one another. Even the most insulated and arbitrary government or system has to be concerned today about the turnings of the popular mind.

THE SAME ACCELERATION IN HISTORY that has produced disarray and irreverence can provide human beings with confidence in their ability to find answers to problems of almost infinite complexity. Progress lies not in the rejection of acceleration but in a proper respect for the possibilities of mind.

PEOPLE MAY DIE OF ILLNESS; they may die of an accident; they may die of old age or starvation or heartbreak. But the idea that a person can be *scheduled* to die—this jabs at the collective mind and causes pain. National boundaries, conflicting ideologies, differences of languages and customs and cultures, all these are transcended when natural law is violated. And the most fundamental of these natural laws is that no agency has the right to *schedule* the death of a human being. When society decides it has the right to kill, then all the members of that society are bound up in the decision. All people are linked to the hand that pulls the final switch, and all must accept part of the responsibility for the acts of their group. The public is essentially the magnification of the individual.

EACH INDIVIDUAL is capable of both great altruism and great venality. He has it within his means to extend the former and exorcise the latter.

The individual is capable of both great compassion and great indifference. He has it within his means to nourish the former and outgrow the latter.

The individual is capable of maintaining great societies and staging great holocausts. He has it within his means to fortify the former and avert the latter.

The individual is capable of ennobling life and disfiguring it. He has it within his means to assert the former and anathematize the latter.

If we recognize that our basic purpose is to justify our humanity, we will have no difficulty in making these essential choices.

PROGRESS PROCEEDS out of elusive but vital fractions. Sudden spurts in the condition of a society come about as the result of small achievements with high symbolic content. The probability of such an upturn may be slight in any given situation. No matter. No one can take the responsibility for assuming it cannot happen. To do otherwise is to hold history in contempt.

"GREAT IDEAS," said Camus, "come into the world as gently as doves. Perhaps, then, if we listen attentively, we shall hear, amid the uproar of empires and nations, a faint flutter of wings, the gentle stirrings of life and hope. Some will say that this hope lies in a nation; others in a man. I believe, rather that it is awakened, revived, nourished by millions of solitary individuals whose deeds and works every day negate frontiers and the crudest implications of history. . . . Each and every man, on the foundation of his own suffering and joys, builds for all."

A FREE SOCIETY cannot long remain free if man is in full retreat from man. For such a society pays a high price if the individual loses faith in his own centrality or in his ability to respond to creative beauty or in the stark fact of his ultimate responsibility. This is a great deal of weight for individual human beings to carry; but if it is political and cultural weightlessness we are seeking, we don't have to get into outer space to find it. We can find it right here on earth and it goes by the name of de-individualization.

PEACE WITHOUT FREEDOM is unthinkable; freedom without peace is impossible. This is one proposition on which conservatives and liberals can agree. Therefore, the making of an enforceable peace that serves the conditions of freedom is at the top of the human agenda.

WISDOM IS NOT MOBILIZED at the same rate as power. The absolutely sovereign state has been far more adept at developing its consciousness of self than its awareness of the human species and its needs. It has put muscle ahead of conscience. Paradoxically, the nation can survive only as it becomes integrated into a larger and more interdependent whole, one that bears some relationship to the totality of the human situation. But the energy and the momentum that are necessary to bring this about can only come from the people themselves, and it is precisely this kind of energy that is wanting because of the weakening of the instinct for survival.

IF THE INSTINCT for human survival is atrophying, where will regeneration come from? It cannot come from the group, however exalted the purpose of the group may be. The hope has to reside where it has always been—with the individual. The challenge here is supremely personal. It does not lend itself to easy superimposition or force-feeding. What the group can do—and it makes little difference whether the group is formally or informally defined—is to arrest its own impatience with the individual long enough to sustain his search for regenerating truths. This is the only way the group is likely to get the truth.

WHAT IS THE ETERNAL and ultimate problem of a free society?

It is the problem of the individual who thinks that one man cannot possibly make a difference in the destiny of that society.

It is the problem of the individual who doesn't really understand the nature of a free society or what is required to make it work.

It is the problem of the individual who has no comprehension of the multiplying power of single but sovereign units.

It is the problem of the individual who regards the act of pulling a single lever in a voting booth in numerical terms rather than historical terms.

It is the problem of the individual who has no real awareness of the millions of bricks that had to be put into place, one by one, over many centuries, in order for him to dwell in the penthouse of freedom. Nor does he see any special obligation to those who continue building the structure or to those who will have to live in it after him, for better or worse.

It is the problem of the individual who recognizes no direct relationship between himself and the decisions made by government in his name. Therefore, he feels no special obligation to dig hard for the information necessary to an understanding of the issues leading to those decisions.

In short, freedom's main problem is the problem of the individual who takes himself lightly historically.

WHO IS THE ENEMY? The enemy is not solely an atomic-muscled totalitarian power with a world ideology.

The enemy is many people. He is a man whose only concern about the world is that it stay in one piece during his own lifetime. He is invariably up to his hips in success and regards his good fortune not as a challenge to get close to the real problems of the age but as proof of the correctness of everything he does. Nothing to him is less important than the shape of things to come or the needs of the next generation. Talk of the legacy of the past or of human destiny leaves him cold. Historically, he is the disconnected man. Hence, when he thinks about the world at all, it is usually in terms of his hope that the atomic fireworks can be postponed for fifteen or twenty years. He is an enemy because nothing less than a passionate concern for the rights of unborn legions will enable the world itself to become connected and whole.

The enemy is a man who not only believes in his own helplessness but actually worships it. His main article of faith is that there are mammoth forces at work which the individual cannot possibly comprehend, much less alter or direct. And so he expends vast energies in attempting to convince other people that there is nothing they can do. He is an enemy because of the proximity of helplessness to hopelessness.

The enemy is a man who has a total willingness to delegate his worries about the world to officialdom. He assumes that only the people in authority are in a position to know and act. He believes that if vital information essential to the making of public decisions is withheld, it can only be for a good reason. If a problem is wholly or partially scientific in nature, he will ask no questions even though the consequences of the problem are political or social.

The enemy is any man in government, high or low, who keeps waiting for a public mandate before he can develop big ideas of his own, but who does little or nothing to bring about such a mandate. Along with this goes an obsessive fear of criticism. To such a man, the worst thing in the world that can happen is to be accused of not being tough-minded in the nation's dealing with other governments. He takes in his stride, however, the accusation that he is doing something that may result in grave injury to the human race.

The enemy is a scientist who makes his calling seem more mysterious than it is, and who allows this mystery to interfere with public participation in decisions involving science or the products of science. His own specialized training may have shielded him from the give-and-take so essential to the democratic process in government.

The enemy is any man in the pulpit who by his words and acts encourages his congregation to believe that the main purpose of the church or the synagogue is to provide social respectability for its members. He talks about the sacredness of life, but he never relates that concept to the real and specific threats that exist today to such sacredness. He identifies himself as a man of God but feels no urge to speak out against a situation in which the nature of man is likely to be altered and cheapened, the genetic integrity of man violated, and distant generations condemned to a lower species. He is a dispenser of balm rather than an awakener of conscience. He is an enemy because the crisis today is as much a spiritual crisis as it is a political one.

NOTHING IS MORE POWERFUL than an individual acting out of his conscience, thus helping to bring the collective conscience to life.

HELPLESSNESS IS THE BASIC PROBLEM. The individual doesn't know where to take hold, or what to do even if he could take hold.

In the time of Pericles, the answer was simple enough. If you were a citizen you went down to the Assembly and stated your case. And if you weren't a citizen you stayed on the sidelines and took your chances. In the time of Jefferson, you could go directly to the Town Meeting or a State Legislature. But today's world is far less cozy. Outlets for concern are far less accessible. The very size of the problem creates its remoteness from the individual. He feels connected to the danger but not to the means of meeting it.

Whatever the worries of the Athenian citizen, or the citizen of the Revolutionary and Constitutional period of American history, the one problem he never had to worry about was human destiny. The question of human destiny may have engaged the philosophical intelligence; it was most certainly a key question in theological thought. But it was not a pressing issue for the individual citizen. Today it is the central issue to which all others are subordinate. The means are now at hand for purging the earth of life in human form or, failing that, to lacerate it so severely that joy will be separated from the human heart. But the individual who wants to do something about it feels cut off and paralyzed.

CERTAIN RIGHTS are acquired by a human being just in the act of being born:

The right to grow and to meet one's individual potentialities.

The right to appraise and apply one's abilities, consistent with the rights of others.

The right to one's thoughts. The right to nourish them and voice them.

The right to make mistakes, whether of thought or deed, without fear of unjust punishment.

The right to hope.

The right to justice, whether the claim is against a person, an aggregation, or government itself.

The right to contemplate human destiny and the mysteries of existence, or to detach oneself altogether from these pursuits.

The right to hold grievances against one's society and to make them known to others.

The right to make a better life for our young.

HUMAN DESPAIR OR DEFAULT can reach a point where even the most stirring visions lose their regenerating and radiating powers. It will be reached only when human beings are no longer capable of calling out to one another, when the words in their poetry break up before their eyes, when their faces become frozen toward their young, and when they fail to make pictures out of clouds racing across the sky.

HOPE CANNOT BE ORDERED INTO BEING. Men in a condition of despair cannot be commanded to generate glorious dreams. But they can be encouraged to rediscover themselves and to be reminded of past achievements under circumstances of enormous difficulty. They can be given confidence in the naturalness of their visions and in the reach of the human mind.

MANY BRAIN RESEARCHERS AGREE there is probably enough reserve capacity in the brain to meet problems far more demanding and complex than any that have so far confronted the species. The fact that most humans do not use more than 15 to 20 percent of their available intelligence seems to indicate that the principal need of humanity is not for a better brain but for some way to make better use of the brains we have.

The concept of reserve brainpower waiting to be unlocked is comforting at a time when philosophers are asking whether the human race is smart enough to survive. The conditions of life have been running down. The dominant intelligence, however, has been trained on tribal business rather than on the operation of human society as a whole. It is possible that this challenge is related to the need for a new consciousness. It is a consciousness that can take into account the condition of the species rather than only the condition of any of its subdivisions.

WHAT IS REQUIRED TODAY is not a catalog of reasons for turning away from people who are in desperate need but a full release of intelligence and ingenuity in facing up to the common interest. The question is not whether our lifeboat can accommodate more survivors but whether, since we are all in the same lifeboat, we can make it safely to shore.

THERE IS A DISPOSITION in some quarters to decry sending food to hungry countries on the grounds that this would only intensify the pressures of the world's population problems. The moment a child is born anywhere in the world he or she has an equal claim on survival and on the compassionate response of the entire human community. Ideas about natural rights, so basic in the American historical experience, must stand on a universal base, or they fall apart completely.

Problems of population pressure are met not by ignoring disease and hunger but by mounting an entirely different kind of offensive—one that educates people and improves their condition.

THE FACT of brotherhood exists. What does not exist is recognition that this is so. Human brotherhood is a biological reality but it does not yet serve as the basis for our day-to-day actions or our working philosophies or our behavior as nations. It is oneness without recognition that defines man's imperfect knowledge of himself and his fellow-man.

THE HUMAN RACE may not be tied together politically or philosophically or culturally, but what all the world's people do have in common is a finite amount of land, an air envelope that is rapidly filling up with filth and poisions, and an uneven water supply that is largely unprotected against infection by sewage and noxious wastes.

The human intelligence that created industrial civilization now has the assignment of making that civilization compatible with man's basic needs. If this is not done, the verdict on man is likely to be that he is a producer of garbage and poisons, and only secondarily a creator of fine works, great deeds, and beauty.

INSTEAD OF FORTIFYING NATURE, we have attacked it with poisons. We have killed off birds that are far more essential to our spirit than our commodities. By going against nature, we have warred against beauty of line, movement, and sound. We have been mucking up our planet, even as we arrogantly go searching for life elsewhere in the universe.

HOW ARE WE TO MEASURE or test a great idea? We measure it by its ability to fit not the needs of the few but of the many. The biggest need of all is to create abundance on earth and use it for the greater good, to eliminate or control the situations that lead to war, whether with respect to predatory assault or the injustice that is worse than war itself. The main job of the next generation must be something more inspiring than clearing away the meaningless rubble left by mighty but mediocre men.

THE INDIVIDUAL who believes he is powerless to affect history marks the beginning of a failure that multiplies itself until it finally takes the form of persons who smash at the very conditions of existence itself. If our philosophers want to summon us to great deeds, let them do it in the name of the institution of humanity.

HUMAN BEINGS have been able to effect vast change, making life different from what it has been before. Our capacity for invention and our sense of creative splendor have constructed great civilizations. But we have never been in command of our own works. We have never been in balance. The result today is that, for all our brilliance, we have thrown ourselves all the way back to our primitive condition, in which our dominant problem was coping with our environment. The difference between our situation today and our tribal beginnings is that the environmental threats today are of our own making. We have been hammering at the chain of life at its weakest link, impairing the ability of the forests and the seas to make oxygen, putting poisons in the air beyond the ability of our lungs to eliminate them, and fouling our soil and water so that they cannot provide us with food.

THE CHALLENGE TO HUMANS in our time is whether they can become aroused not just over small but over large dangers, whether they can perceive universal problems as well as personal ones, whether they can become as concerned over their survival as a species as they are over their jobs.

A WORLD CONSENSUS has never before been necessary. But we are living in a new and different world, a world that has suddenly become a single geographic unit. Such a world, in order to function safely and responsibly, needs all the thought and attention it can get. People of ideas now have to operate on a world stage. They must find their way to each other across national barriers. They must not hesitate to proclaim their allegiance to the human family. They must make the human interest their prime concern, working with the sovereignties if possible and against them if necessary. Human destiny is the first responsibility of responsible men. This is the first cause. With peace, all problems are soluble. Without it, nothing is safe.

THE HUMAN RACE is in jeopardy whenever power, insensitivity, and ignorance are joined together.

DESPITE THE HISTORIANS, there has been only one age of man. It is the age of primitive man. The beginning of the age of civilized man, when it comes, will be marked by his political, philosophical, and spiritual awareness of himself as a member of a world species with world needs and with the capacity and desire to create world institutions to meet those needs. Humankind need not sacrifice the nation to create such institutions. It need only recognize and assert an allegiance of humans to one another beyond national boundaries and to do those things in the human interest that the nation as an organization is incapable of doing.

BELONGING TO A NATION, man has nations that can speak for him. Belonging to a religion, man has religions that can speak for him. Belonging to an economic and social order, man has economic and political orders that can speak for him. But belonging to the human race, man is without a spokesman.

WE JUSTIFY THE GIFT OF LIFE in many ways: by our awareness of its preciousness and its fragility; by developing to the fullest the sensitivies and potentialities that come with it; by putting the whole of our intelligence to work in sustaining and enhancing the conditions that make it possible; by cherishing the human habitat; and by removing the obstructions in our access to and trust in one another.

THERE ARE NO LIMITS to man's ability to respond to appeals made to his natural goodness. It is doubtful whether there is any greater power in human affairs than is exerted through the example of man's love for man.

NATURAL RIGHTS presuppose natural options. It is part of human uniqueness that we are endowed with the faculty of choice. We are not entirely helpless in the eternal struggle between good and evil that exists both outside us and within us. If the choice is the right one, then an element of progress has come into the world. In fact, progress may be just another way of saying that enough people have chosen wisely between good and evil and that these decisions have had their effects.

HUMANS ARE NOT HELPLESS. They have never been helpless. They have only been deflected or deceived or dispirited.

LIFE IS an adventure in forgiveness.

HOPE MAY BE FORTIFIED by experience but that is not where it begins. It begins in the certainty that things can be done that have never been done before. This is the ultimate reality and it defines the uniqueness of the human mind.

THE GREATEST OF ALL historical truths is represented by the ability of human beings to exercise their moral imagination. Theories about human helplessness, therefore, have no standing in history.

IS IT POSSIBLE that we don't give birth to ideals or visions? Is it possible that they constantly exist but that we discover them only when we are prepared to accept them?

THE EGO CAN BECOME DANGEROUS when inflamed—dangerous to the individual and society. But a person's ego is necessary. It is a source of pride. It is the basis of personal achievement. It is a fundamental resource of human progress. Human beings need to be recognized; they need to be known by their good works; they need to be loved. In all these respects, the ego is important and indispensable. The concept of brotherhood would be impossible without it, for no person can truly know love for others unless he can respond to it himself. But if the ego governs absolutely, then a person loses his vital balance and is ruled solely by his own tastes and needs—and becomes hostile to his own nature.

CONVICTIONS ARE POTENT only when they are shared. Until then, they are merely a form of daydreaming.

ANY ASPECT of dualism in man creates problems, whether it be good versus evil, altruism versus selfishness, cooperativeness versus competitiveness, or cowardice versus courage. But it is also part of our uniqueness that we are endowed with the faculty of choice.

STUDENTS OF HUMAN BEHAVIOR don't exhaust themselves trying to determine whether man is inherently good or evil; they concentrate on the conditions that make it possible for the good to emerge and the evil to be arrested.

LEISURE TIME in the contemporary world is potentially the greatest gift to the individual yet it is also a problem of ghastly dimensions. It has thrown man out of joint. People have more time on their hands than their knowledge, interests, or aptitudes can accommodate. Newly available hours sometimes lead man to helplessness and foundering than to creative discovery. Retirement, supposedly a cherished opportunity to join the winner's circle, can be more dangerous than automobiles or LSD. It can be a consignment to no-man's land. It is the gleaming brass ring that unhorses the rider.

SILENCE MUST BE COMPREHENDED as not solely the absence of sound. It is the natural environment for serenity and contemplation. Life without silence is life without privacy. The difference between sanity and madness is the quality of our thoughts. Silence is on the side of sanity.

OUR OWN AGE is not likely to be distinguished in history for the large numbers of people who insisted on finding time to think. Plainly, this is not the Age of the Meditative Man. It is a sprinting, squinting, shoving age. Substitutes for repose are a billion-dollar business. Almost daily, new antidotes for contemplation spring into being and leap out from store counters. Silence, already the world's most critical shortage, is in danger of becoming a nasty word. Modern man may or may not be obsolete, but he is certainly wired for sound and he twitches as naturally as he breathes.

THERE IS NO COSMIC HOCUS-POCUS that dictates that time will always serve the cause of reason. Time by itself is supremely indifferent to the petty and major problems that beset the human race. If the circumstances favor progress, time favors progress. If the circumstances favor disintegration, time favors disintegration. The job of truly reasonable persons is to create and enlarge those conditions which make progress possible, and to arrest or change those conditions which make disintegration inevitable.

THE EARLIEST GREEK BOOK of which there is a historical record, Hesiod's *Works and Days,* cried out for a return to the good old days, when life was less complicated and more trusting and when, presumably, one's illusions were intact. This is the way the remote but remembered past tends to appear to the present. Retrospect imparts a quality of innocence to bygone times.

THE VAUNTED military power of ancient Athens has long since disappeared. But the ideas of that civilization have proved far more durable than its fighting ships. The words of Aristotle and Plato stand even taller and more powerful today than they did twenty-four hundred years ago.

WE ARE LEFT WITH a crisis in decision. The main test before us involves our will to change rather than our ability to change.

NOTHING ABOUT HUMAN LIFE is more precious than that we can define our own purpose and shape our own destiny.

TO SAY THAT MAN DOES NOT LIVE by bread alone does not meet the larger question: What is it that he does live by? Whatever the full and rounded equation will show, it is possible that one of the factors is vital purpose. Can the pain of discontent be relieved without some idea of what man's goals are or ought to be? It is not what we have or do not have but where we want to go that represents the test of sanity. The measure of greatness, for the individual or the nation, is not just where we have been but where we want to go.

HISTORY IS an accumulation of errors.

THE ULTIMATE ADVENTURE on earth is the adventure of ideas.

"HISTORY," wrote Edmund Burke, "is full of momentous tri-fles—the accident which kills or preserves in life some figure of destiny; the weather on some critical battlefield, like the fog at Lutzen or the sun at Towton; the change of wind which brings two fleets to a decisive action . . . the birth or the death of a child; a sudden idea which results in some potent invention." Bertrand Russell echoed this thought when he wrote that "so many circumstances of a small and accidental nature are rele-vant, that no broad and simple uniformities are possible."

LOVERS OF ideological battle cries like to think that the French Revolution was primarily the product of passionate words attached to a passionate cause, but in actuality the greatest sin-gle impetus behind that event was the unpredictable crop fail-ure of 1788. One wonders what would have happened if F.D.R. had lived only a few months longer. Would the atomic bomb have been dropped on Hiroshima? Would the world be caught up in a nuclear arms race? Some questions, as F.D.R. himself said, are too "iffy" to be taken seriously. Even so, one wonders.

THE SAFE PASSAGE of human beings through history calls for at least as much attention as is now given to passengers in flight.

AT SOME POINT the human race must have its innings. An assess-ment must ultimately be made in terms of human develop-ment. In the end, it is not the nation but humans who will have to account for the record of life on earth.

FREEDOM IS the highest prize on this earth. It is also the most precarious and fragile.

ANY LIFE, however long, is too short if the mind is bereft of splendor, the passions underworked, the memories sparse, and the imagination unlit by radiant musings.

OUR PHILOSOPHERS and scholars and educators should be among the first to recognize that in a crisis of ideas the biggest ideas are the most needed ones.

4

Options in Jeopardy

MAN GOES INTO HIS LABORATORY and comes out with a device that has stamped upon it a death warrant for at least a billion persons. The device makes it possible to expunge in a fraction of a second what it has taken two thousand years to put together piece by piece. The device is not created on an empty and tranquil stage. It is presented against a background of lit fuses and supercharged tensions. Yet nothing explodes in our minds. The device can rock the earth, but it has yet to make a dent in our thinking.

IN THE CONTROL ROOM OF A CYCLOTRON, about a year after the bombing of Hiroshima: Here, inside this shed, a new environment for human beings is being shaped, made possible by a successful invasion of nature's innermost fortress, the atom. There is only one trouble with this new environment: It requires the perfect man. Only the perfect man—perfect morally, politically, ideologically, and spiritually—could avail himself of all the benefits in the atomic cornucopia. Only the perfect man would be capable of operating a society in which atomic energy could eliminate want, destroy disease, and provide for a rich and purposeful existence. But to talk about the need for perfection in humans is to talk about the need for another species. The essence of a human being is imperfection. Imperfection and blazing contradictions—between good and evil, altruism and selfishness, cooperativeness and combativeness, optimism and fatalism, affirmation and negation. The challenge is to make the world safe for our imperfections and our contradictions, to keep our differences from catching on fire.

THE SENSE OF PERSONAL REGENERATION in post-war Hiroshima is discernible and unmistakable. We find not only proof of the power of life over death but of the individual discovery of such physical, emotional, and spiritual resources as even philosophers have not dared to dream. This regeneration has soared far beyond personal rehabilitation to a restoration of vital faith in human destiny. Today there is a new vision in Hiroshima. It is that the city has a mission to explain itself to the world, to offer itself as a laboratory specimen in the making of world peace.

WE ARE ALL ABOARD THE SAME FLIGHT. The plane is called the nuclear age. What makes the situation precarious is that there is audible snarling from the direction of the pilots struggling over the controls. One thing is certain. They cannot grapple with one another and keep their hands on the controls at the same time.

WE TALK OF "CLEAN" HYDROGEN BOMBS as though we are dealing with the ultimate in moral refinement. What kind of monstrous imagination is it that connects the word "clean" to a device that will put a torch to civilization? What the world is waiting for is not a better way to make a "clean" hydrogen explosive but a better way to get rid of dirty wars.

THE LINE BETWEEN ULTIMATE ABSURDITY and reality is getting thinner all the time. What gives our age its bitter flavor is precisely the triumph of irrational behavior in the operation of society. Total power is being wedded to total madness. The official delusion persists that we can buy security with superbombs. What we are buying instead is a colossal suicide pact.

IF NUCLEAR WAR SHOULD OCCUR, it will come about not because it was inevitable, but because not enough men took the trouble to avert it. It will be a grim reflection not on the inexorability of history, but on the low value we place on the uniqueness of human life.

THINK OF A PERSON. Think of someone, living or dead, whose life has enriched your own. Think back for a moment on the name or names that have given history a forward thrust, a sense of direction, an encounter with the beautiful. Names connected to great ideas or causes or deeds or works of art.

An intimate relationship, all at once, has come to exist between the lives of such persons and your own. The turn of events has made you the custodian of all their works. It is now in your power—power on a scale never before possessed by human beings—to protect and fulfill those great works and ideas, or to shatter them beyond recognition or repair. There is no achievement in human experience, no record, no thing of beauty that cannot now be rescinded and all of its benefits and traces swept into a void. It is this that distinguishes our generation from all previous generations: We possess total authority not only over our own time but over all the ages and works of man. Earlier generations have had the power merely to affect history; ours has the power to expunge it.

NOTHING IS MORE ARROGANT than pronouncements by government officials about "permissible levels" of radioactive poisons in the human body. The proper amount of strontium 90 in the human body is no strontium 90.

THERE IS SCOPE for neither ideological fulfillment nor national purpose in nuclear suicide.

NEVER IN HISTORY has the sovereign state been more powerful or less secure. Its capacity for waging war has never been so great nor its ability to protect itself so puny. We cannot invoke irrational force as the principal way of achieving rational restraint.

THE TERM "national security" has a built-in contradiction. In the atomic age, no *national* security is possible. Either we have a workable world security system or we have nothing. The efforts of the individual nations to achieve military supremacy or even adequacy are actually competitive and provocative in their effect.

NONE OF THE OLD QUESTIONS—United States versus Soviet Union, the world balance-of-power struggle, the Middle East contentions—are capable any longer of being resolved by force, although they gravitate generally to force. But at least there is a new sense in the world that confrontations must not take a nuclear form. But that realization must be accompanied by an equal determination to create the means by which confrontations cannot merely be avoided but resolved. It becomes necessary, therefore, to create the global institutions and, more importantly, the global philosophy, that cannot just regulate the animosities but can dissolve them.

ONE OF THE GREAT DANGERS confronting the world is that the men who have devised the new poison gases or the new explosives or who have been producing bacteriological weapons may not be content to see their work go forever unused. These men are not brutes bent on projecting their aggressive natures onto the society of nations. These men have been placed in a position where they are compelled to deal with existing conditions and the logic that seems to them to issue therefrom. Their rendezvous, as they see it, is not with destiny but with inevitability. The essential evil, of course, resides in the failure of people everywhere to think through the implications of a new age that has made the world a geographic unit without also making it a governed unit.

The men who preside over the new weapons do so inside a certain context. Our job is to change the context.

PEOPLE SPECULATE on the horrors that would be let loose by nuclear war. Some of the worst horrors are already here. The transformation today of otherwise decent people into death-calculating machines; the psychological reconditioning for an age of cannibalism; the wholesale premeditation of murder and the acceptable conditions thereof; the moral insolence of those who presume to prescribe the circumstances under which it is spiritually permissible to kill one's neighbors; the desensitization of human response to pain; the acquiescence in the inevitability of disaster; the cheapening of human personality with its concomitant, irresponsible fatalism—all these are part of an already existing, fast-swelling chamber of horrors.

WE LIVE A LIFE of compartmentalization; some sections are marked with glittering splendor; others remain as they were thousands of years ago. We are still bound to dangerously primitive ideas. Nothing in history can begin to compare with the present spectacle of a world drifting toward a possible war of hydrogen bombs with little general realization of the need for people to transcend their petty problems and dedicate themselves to the building of a structure of world law.

In the past the world didn't merely slough off its primitive ideas or stumble out of them. The defeat of a delusion was generally the result of courageous response to courageous leadership. A few great men were unafraid to appeal directly to the good sense and quality of integrity that are deep within most men and that have only to be awakened in order to constitute the strongest force known in history.

ALMOST EVERYWHERE WE LOOK, ideas hostile to the human potential are springing up. These ideas are defeatist. They enfeeble man by taking away his tomorrow. They scorn hope and they kill purpose. They are cold and impersonal. The future is difficult enough without depriving man of his will to endure, to sustain and be sustained.

THE EASIEST WAY for a nation to destroy itself is to make national security the highest value. Indeed, people are never more insecure than when they become obsessed with their fears at the expense of their dreams, or when the ability to fight becomes more important than the things worth fighting for.

THE NOTION that we can best cope with threats to our security or to world security by setting up vast cloak-and-dagger operations, or by creating authority outside the framework of the constitutional government, is itself a threat to the freedom of the American people. We cannot engage in subversion abroad without subverting the history and institutions of the United States.

THE UNITED STATES GOVERNMENT was designed by thinkers who knew that men and raw power don't go together. This to them was the most important lesson in history. The Philadelphia Constitutional Convention was an exercise in the control and distribution of power. More than any collective undertaking in history, that convention tried to create a structure of government in which even the best men would be kept separated from power that could be used capriciously or willfully and therefore dangerously. The best way to protect citizens against abuses of power by men in government is to circumscribe the power, define it, refine it, subordinate it to law and due process. This design was good enough to create a system of government that has been in continuous operation longer than any other in the world.

THE MAIN PROBLEM is how to keep the human race alive at a time when every facility and skilled knowledge are being mobilized to eliminate it or change it. The most significant thing about this problem is that almost everyone recognizes it exists but almost no one has any idea where to take hold in order to deal with it.

THE ONLY POSSIBLE JUSTIFICATION TODAY for military preparedness is the prevention of war. If war should break out, the military policy will have failed. Its principal function will have been shattered—along with everything else.

THE ISSUE IS NOT whether one side can impose its will on the other but how we can keep both sides from fusing an atomic incinerator.

IF I BELIEVED that peace could be achieved only at the expense of principle, I would be against peace. If I believed that peace meant surrender to evil, I would be against peace. I say this though I have seen an atomic bomb explode sixteen miles away, though I have seen dozens of dead cities, their insides hollowed out by dynamite and fire, though I have seen the faces of the dead in war. But the transcendent truth is that a meaningful and creative peace *is* possible and that it is within our means to fashion a world which is safe and fit for human beings.

AT THE HEART OF THE THEORY of deterrent force is the belief that a potential enemy will be disinclined to attack if he knows the counterattack will be immediate and devastating. The main flaw in the deterrent theory, however, is that it does not deter. It is natural for a nation to display not restraint, but a willingness to march to the brink when its national interests are threatened. Far from inspiring great restraints, the deterrent produces jitters and hair triggers.

THE HUMAN CRISIS in today's world is represented not primarily by competing ideologies, but by power without control. The competition between ideologies is real, but this competition has existed in various forms throughout most of history. Superimposed upon the present clash of ideologies is the new fact that man is in possession of almost total power but his instruments of control over that power are unscientific and indeed primitive.

The question that cannot be avoided is whether any nation, even in its own defense, has the right to destroy the rest of the world.

THE FRUSTRATION AND TORMENT of coping with a billowing crisis has already led a few hotheads to go browsing through the bargain-basement counters of catastrophes for ready-made solutions. We are spending millions on civil defense and other measures that are as outmoded as a knight's suit-of-armor in front of a howitzer. The raw fact is that our cities are indefensible.

TWENTIETH-CENTURY HUMANS will find their greatness not in a bomb shelter but out in the open where they belong. We will achieve our moment of triumph on earth not by proving that we can emerge from a dungeon after our civilization has been obliterated, but by eliminating war and the evils that lead to war.

IF WE WOULD MAKE SENSE out of our lives, we can only begin by asserting a collective responsibility to match collective power. The world has been superbly organized for everything except the life of the human race. The knowledge and the means have been assembled to turn the world into a radioactive wasteland. But there has been no comparable collective effort to govern the relations of nations or to make them truthful and responsible or to keep them from becoming inimical to life. Even if we do not succeed overnight in accomplishing this purpose, the fact that we can identify it as a prime need and are prepared to talk about it might do some good.

FEW THEMES have challenged the thoughts of philosophers throughout the ages more than the idea of the fragility of human life. Even a drop of water, says Pascal, can suffice to destroy a man. But now, at the culmination of a century of science, we also ponder the fragility of civilization.

If human history is now drawing to a close, it is not so much because of malevolence or incompetence deep within the species but because the human mind seems unable to convince itself that its own destiny is the issue.

AN AMERICAN demonstrates his patriotism not by pressuring for nuclear showdowns or by fast-and-loose talk about dropping hydrogen bombs but by tapping and putting to work the deepest wisdom human history has to offer. A new kind of force must be created which, when fully used, can safeguard this nation and its freedom and make a contribution to world peace in general.

THE ANSWER TO DRIFT IS DIRECTION. The answer to insanity is sanity. If the energy, money, and resources that went into air-raid shelters were put to work in the making of a better world, we would do far more to safeguard the American future than all the underground holes that could be built in one thousand years. And if we are serious about shelters, let us make the United Nations into a shelter broad enough and deep enough to sustain an enforced peace under law. The war has not yet begun. Freedom, however abused, still exists. Perhaps we can use that freedom to rally enough peoples around the idea of a world under law.

IF A HISTORIAN should be among the survivors of another war, he would have no shortage of material for his chapter on the way attitudes led to consequences. He would find it significant that the catastrophe did not overtake peoples without warning but that almost everyone had a vivid idea that something was wrong, that the means were at hand for crushing the human race and scattering the architecture of human civilization. This historian would find it remarkable that such knowledge did not produce wisdom, that the finest communications system ever devised in human history produced neither a basic understanding of the issues nor the desire to act on them.

THE PROBLEM—that of trying to halt the spread of nuclear weapons to many nations—is not solely how to keep the genie from escaping from the bottle. The problem is what to do about the dinosaur mentality in our midst.

If the President of the United States is weighed down by genies bursting out of bottles and dinosaurs prancing on the lawn, the antidote will have to come not from court wizards but from an alert, rational, and responsible populace. If enough people can mobilize enough energy to communicate their concern, the terrible loneliness of the Presidency on this important issue may be eased.

Ultimately, the future of the nation rests where it began—in the ability of its citizens to stay on top of the big issues, retaining those men who serve them best and throwing out the others.

RIGHT HERE ON EARTH is the place to do something about our main problems. Otherwise we may find that astronauts will roam outer space in heavenly splendor with nothing to come back to.

IN TODAY'S WORLD the governing facts are not always tidy and logical, but they are the facts that spell the difference between life and death.

WE ARE MAKING OUR PEACE WITH LUNACY. We are coping with enveloping madness by becoming a part of it. We fiercely preserve all our competitive instincts, but make expendable our ability to reason and make moral judgments. We take dangerous nonsense in our stride. We detach ourselves from the lessons of history.

LIFE THAT IS TENTATIVE has a tendency to become cheap. What does it mean to live in an age when the defensive level of human beings has been reduced to that of insects against a blowtorch? The most enshrined phrase in the lexicon of philosophers is "the dignity of man," yet dignity does not depend only on political characters or declarations. Dignity also means solidity; it means a moral contract accepting life as infinitely precious. How much reverence for life is possible when everyone knows that the flick of a finger can incinerate a billion human beings and that a nod can release tons of disease germs? A painful world man can train himself to endure, but a world that on the whim of a madman can become a crematorium or a disease chamber—this is the giant thief that steals a man's dignity and his reverence for life.

WAR IS NOT INEVITABLE. It is possible; it may even be probable; but it need not be inevitable.

EVERYONE UNDERSTANDS what happens when the machinery of law in a small community suddenly breaks down, but there is no comparable awareness of the dangers that confront every member of the human species because of the absence of law binding on nations. No rational process now exists, therefore, for assuring the basic safety of the human species. We stumble into the future day-to-day, dependent more on the hope that our margin for error may not have been completely used up than on a working design for a peaceful world.

IF NATIONS LIVE IN ANARCHY the individual citizen pays the price of anarchy. Law and order within the nation are no protection against the larger violence and injustice outside the nation. Whatever the intermediate form of protection afforded to man in daily life, the major threats to his well-being and future find him open and exposed.

A CONSENSUS IN FAVOR of a governed world is not going to take place overnight. But everything begins with advocacy and debate. Just in the process of arguing the great ideas, a new context for the human situation begins to emerge.

THE UNITED NATIONS should not be the last thing that statesmen think of when the peace is threatened but the first. Each time the United Nations is bypassed or sidetracked or overlooked its heartbeat becomes a little weaker. The cause of the United Nations is inseparable from the cause of peace. But we will not have peace by afterthought. If the United Nations is to survive, those who represent it must bolster it, those who advocate it must submit to it, and those who believe in it must fight for it.

FOR THE UNITED STATES to discover its greatest power, it has only to regard itself as an instrument through which the ennoblement of man may be served. We can declare that we will not fire into the body of mankind in the pursuit of our own security. We can say our purpose is to use human knowledge and energy in creating the finest life of which the human imagination is capable. We can make our voice the most resonant in the world behind the idea of world law—an idea that may yet create the conditions that alone can give reasonable assurance of peace and freedom.

WAR IS AN INVENTION of the human mind. The human mind can invent peace.

MAN IS COMPLETELY DARING and inventive about the feasibility of a world holocaust but absurdly timid and unresourceful about the making of a world community. He denies oneness of hope but asserts the oneness of despair. Unity of spirit is resisted; unity of defeat is pursued.

THE WORLD CRISIS is created not just by the explosive atom but by inadequate means of controlling international lawlessness. Control is inoperable without power, power is dangerous without law, and law is impossible without government.

ABSOLUTE POWER and absolute nonsense are being wedded to one another in the modern world. If this is to be changed, some nation will have to come forward with a prescription that fits the needs of a human society in quest of sanity. The prescription will have to look beyond unfettered national sovereignty to a condition of effective law. It is barely possible, even at this late date, that the prescription might serve as a powerful rallying point for what may well be the last stand of the thinking man in this corner of the universe.

IT IS THIS that all human beings share today—the emergence of a common destiny and the beginning of a perception, however misty, that something beyond the nation will have to be brought into being if the human race is to have any meaning.

THE HEART OF THE MATTER is that the struggle between the United States and the Soviet Union is rooted not in ideology but in world anarchy. The irony is that insecurity in the United States about the Soviet Union is bound to grow in direct proportion to the Soviet Union's departure from its traditional Communist aims and methods. For the Soviet Union will become stronger as she veers away from Communism. And the stronger the Soviet Union becomes, the more apprehensive we ourselves become about our own position in the world. There is no use in blinking at the facts. The fully sovereign nation is the enemy of human life. The difficulty in achieving world government is the worst of all possible reasons for not dedicating ourselves to it.

IT HAS REMAINED for our age to provide the most primitive and dangerous idea ever held by the mind of man. This is the idea that it is somehow possible to preserve human civilization on this earth in the present condition of world anarchy. Distant generations may find it even stranger that men of standing in theology and philosophy should have spent their time spinning elaborate theories about the uniqueness of Western Civilization instead of pursuing the necessary philosophy of the whole.

THE SURPRISING THING ABOUT contemporary human society is that it has laboriously worked out techniques for coping with the erratic behavior of citizens but then completely sets these techniques aside for dealing with the erratic behavior of nations. The machinery of law is the only effective means developed during history for dealing with private conflicts of vital interests, yet the machinery of law has yet to be created for dealing with conflicts when they reach national and nuclear proportions. Against this background, we cannot regard ourselves as educated so long as we are detached from this particular lesson of history.

THE PRIME FACT of our time is that the sovereign nations have gone berserk, pursuing measures that are leading to a hideous assault on human life. For all our inventiveness, we are still primitive when it comes to designing and operating collective organisms.

IT IS NOT CORRECT to say that Americans and Soviets cannot see things the same way. Both insist that the people on the other side are able to understand only the language of force. Because of this, human history may be drawing to a close. The Soviet citizen who claims he is helpless to act at least has a totalitarian society as an excuse. What excuse do Americans have?

NO NATION, however efficient its soundproofing mechanism, can be deaf to the reverberations of world opinion on the requirements of human survival. Nothing is more mysterious in human affairs than the penetrating power of great ideas.

NATIONS EXHIBIT ALL the variable characteristics of people. Some of them have been content with modest size and achievements, eager to live quietly and sensitively. Others have been acquisitive and insatiable, noisy and obnoxious.

DESPITE THE WIDE RANGE of collective behavior, one historic fact emerges. The larger a nation, the more certain it is to get involved in traffic problems with other large nations. Like an individual, the nation seeks economic power and prosperity; but unlike the individual, it is not restrained by properly constituted agencies of law as it goes about advancing its interests. Inevitably, those interests come into conflict with others.

TRUE SECURITY begins with the knowledge that no great national edifices are going to be built on a foundation of universal suicide.

THE GREAT DANGER is that the mistakes of the past will go unrecognized. Human beings can survive anything except ignored and unredeemed tragedy.

WHEN WORLD LAW was first mentioned, people said it was too soon. Now when it is mentioned, they say it is too late. It is neither too soon nor too late. If we have a voice and an idea behind it, and if what we say makes sense, the time is just right.

WORLD PEACE will not be achieved by drift or default. The goal must be defined, the approaches must be accepted, the responsibilities must be fixed.

MORE AND MORE, the choice for the world's people is between becoming world warriors and world citizens.

STATESMEN CRY "Peace, peace," but there is no peace because they will not accept the slightest restraint on their ability to roam and fend at will in the world or to do anything they conceive to be in their own national interest, even though what they are doing may be contrary to every known canon of justice and decency.

THE UNITED NATIONS cannot survive as a cockpit in which to choose up sides or to trade insults and abuse. It must be vested with objective standards for establishing justice in the relations among nations. Most important, it must represent peoples, not just governments.

MEN CAUGHT UP IN GAMES of international realpolitik tend to delude themselves with the thought that "hard" matters of military policy are the only ones that count. History, however, is littered with the relics of civilizations whose leaders felt uncomfortable or scornful in the presence of moral questions.

EVERY MAJOR PROBLEM in the world today calls for a world response. It is impossible, in fact, to think seriously about such problems without recognizing that they all point to the need for transforming the United Nations into a series of effective authorities, as part of a world organization with law-making and law-enforcing powers. Moreover, it is difficult to see how the world can feed itself adequately, or how the arms race can be halted, or how we can keep outer space from becoming a nuclear shooting gallery, or how we can keep the world's air and water from becoming poisoned, or how we can head off the predatory competition among nations for ownership of the resources of the seas, or new sources of energy available on a large scale can be developed, unless the United Nations is made into an effective organization with primary responsibility for the conditions of life on planet Earth.

NO NATION OR PEOPLE enjoys a dispensation against disaster. Survival depends less on ideas than on action. The nation, or rather the people, that will define the ideal of a world government backed by the spirit of universalism as a basis both for survival and fulfillment will attract to itself such massed support everywhere as will dissolve what now appear to be the ineradicable components of disaster.

AN IDEAL IS GOING BEGGING—the ideal of world citizenship. Milton, Paine, Hugo, Heine, Tennyson, and numberless others were eloquent in their plea for a world citizenship. Today the basic fundamentals for the ideal exist, but the ideal itself is virtually an orphan. Can it be that one of the greatest obstacles to world citizenship today is the lack of awareness that the ideal is not only possible but mandatory?

A LAW THAT CAN HELP to control the acquisition of a gun by an individual is logical enough, but what about the logic that makes it possible for major nations to have their salesmen traveling around the world with bargain offerings of guns and bullets by the millions along with fighting planes, tanks, howitzers, and hundreds of other items that can kill on a mass scale? Is it only madness in the singular that concerns us?

It will be increasingly difficult for any society to demand morality and respect for life in its citizens in the absence of such morality in the affairs of nations.

IN AN ENVIRONMENT OF VIOLENCE, life becomes not only tentative but cheap. The sense of beauty, the capacity to be awakened and enlarged by a tender experience, the possibilities for compassionate thought—all these are being crowded and pressured by the language of force. The mind of man is rapidly being hammered out of shape by the constant pounding of explosive accusations, denunciations, and vilifications—all tied to the casual and precipitate use of force.

Nothing multiplies more easily than force. Whatever man's other shortages—food, learning, work—he has no shortage of devices or instruments for expressing his raw anger. Guns have a way of materializing more readily than the commodities that sustain life or the undertakings that dignify or enlarge it.

In its grossest and most lethal form, force is represented by groupings of people into nations. This makes possible a concentration of collective effort with a minimum of restraint and a maximum of fury. Any one of five such major groupings in today's world possesses enough force to squash all life. They are piling up explosive upon explosive as though the test of a nation is not how much sanity and progress it can provide for its citizens but how much devastation it can carry out in their name. At least two of these groupings are breeding and accumulating vast stores of bacteriological organisms that could make of the earth's people a retching, writhing mass of diseased and helpless creatures.

NATIONS TRADITIONALLY are incapable of dealing sensibly with insults or assaults. Their tendency is to respond with such severity that the offending nation will not be tempted to repeat the abuse. Everyone believes in the same system; therefore it cannot work. Each nation wants to teach the other nation a lesson. This kind of education is unproductive and explosive.

IT IS A CURIOUS PHENOMENON of nature that only two species practice the art of war—men and ants, both of which, ironically, maintain complex social organizations. Both these species employ massed numbers in violent combat; both rely on strategy and tactics to meet developing situations or to capitalize on the weaknesses in the strategy and tactics of the other side. The longest continuous war ever fought between men lasted thirty years. The longest ant war ever recorded lasted six and a half weeks, or whatever the corresponding units would be in ant reckoning.

IF THE EXISTENCE of force can no longer serve as the main source of a nation's security, something else will have to take its place if the human society is to be able to endure and function. The new power that must be brought into being is the power represented by human will—the power of consensus. Out of it can come the energy and momentum for building a haven for human society.

EVERY MALEVOLENT IDEA about producing mass suffering is given sanction the moment the word security is affixed to it. Thus, it is considered proper and essential to mass-produce odorless and invisible gases that can inflict heart attacks, or bombs that can disseminate germs to spread the very diseases that mankind over countless generations has been trying to eliminate. But nothing is more insidious in this apocalyptic inventory than the determination of each side to convince the other that it would not have the slightest hesitation to turn it all loose in any confrontation.

IT IS precisely because we react on the level of tribal warriors, ignoring our membership in and obligation to the society of humans as a whole—it is precisely because of this that we have separated ourselves from the wisdom of what is required to achieve genuine security and fulfill the promise of a better world.

SOME GOVERNMENT OFFICIALS seem more concerned about the fact that other nations may not respect our strength than they are about the fact that other nations may not respect our wisdom.

THE PRIME FAILURE of modern society is that it has neither the philosophy nor the institutions to deal with crimes against humanity itself. Public fear and indignation are aroused by palpable things—a woman assaulted in a doorway, the hijacking of a plane, the terrorist bombings of a school bus, Watergates. But the conversion of masses of men into killers, the disfiguration of human values on a mammoth scale by governments themselves, the diversion of natural resources and human energies into the means of senseless total destruction, the assault on the conditions of life, the puncturing of the ozone layer—these are towering crimes. The failure to see them as such is a danger in itself.

HISTORY IS SHAPED as much by intangibles as by hard facts. The biggest changes of the twentieth century were not foreseen by the experts. They had no way of anticipating the tides of political change that were to sweep over the world. They had no way of knowing where or how human hopes or fears would be suddenly created into vast surges of energy that would transform political, economic, and social institutions.

Obviously, the intangibles can be bad as well as good. No one predicted that the economic and social chaos in Germany after the First World War would produce an Adolf Hitler and a war that would take sixty million lives. The attempted conquest of Europe by Nazi Germany, however, was ultimately blocked by an intangible known as the human spirit. The magic of Winston Churchill's words enabled the British people to persevere at a time when many experts believed their defeat was inevitable.

IF EVERYONE ON EARTH were to stop everything in order to focus on the madness of the nuclear-arms race, some sanity might yet emerge that could lead to safety.

5

Freedom as Teacher

THE DEMOCRATIC FAITH is based not as much upon the assumption of leadership by the few as upon the wisdom and conscience of the many. When the groundswell generated thereby becomes manifest, there will be a magnificent connecting-up between man and his governors and, what is more important, between man and man.

THE MEN WHO FASHIONED THE DESIGN for America's political structure could not guarantee that it would have total continuity and stability. They assumed that every now and then great tremors would occur. Their hope, however, was that no single man or party could knock the structure down. They took change for granted, and they never made the mistake of assuming that all change was for the better. They tried to keep change from being frozen in any one direction. And they tried to provide the mechanism of an inner balance that would act against any fundamental dislocation of the main uprights.

This theory of the inner balance is about to be tested as it has never been tested before. There is every reason to welcome such a test.

TWO HUNDRED YEARS AGO, a great nation was founded on the idea that the strength of a country begins with moral concepts, the truth of which is confirmed in the natural response of human beings and in the history of the race. If we want that nation to go on for another two hundred years, we will dispense with the nonsense that moral values are incidental and that the national interest can stand apart from the human interest.

THE YOUNG AMERICAN GIANTS who designed the government of the United States knew how to put men and ideas together.

They connected their spiritual beliefs to political action. Like the philosopher-statesmen of ancient Greece, they sought perfection through an integrated wholeness. They had a zest for life. They helped to educate one another. They combined moral imagination with a flair for leadership. They provided their age with an infusion of intellectual energy, a rising sense of conviction that there were wrongs to be set right, and that the moment was now. They found the right words. The precise phrases of the Declaration of Independence occurred to many men almost at the same time, all of them experiencing the shock of recognition when they discovered they were not alone.

DEMOCRACY IS THE ONLY political philosophy that entitles and enables the individual to say "no" to government—and get away with it. Indeed, the one word most expressive of democracy is "no." Democracy says "no" to the government that would invade the natural rights of the individual or the group. It says "no" to the government that would push people around, even though this may mean that the people push the government around. The American Constitution is more specific concerning what shall not be part of the structure of government than it is concerning what shall. The words "no" and "not" are conspicuous in every article and section. Nowhere are those two words more in evidence than in the Bill of Rights.

THE GOVERNMENT OF THE UNITED STATES was conceived by men who believed it possible for a nation to become a moral instrument. They rejected the notion of a double standard under which the state can itself be immoral, mendacious, brutal, or irrational while demanding that its citizens adhere to a code of responsibility and reason. That noble conception of the American Founding Fathers, however, has no standing in today's world. The national sovereign state not only relies on force but resists every effort to replace force with workable codes of law. Available force now amounts to an equivalent of thirty thousand pounds of TNT for every human being on earth. Nothing else is produced by man in such abundance. This force, if used, could make the world a desolate waste. Even without being used, nuclear explosives shape the morality, or lack of it, of nations. In their dealings with each other, the sovereign nations do not hesitate to lie, cheat, and be short-tempered and abusive.

AMERICA THRIVES ON CONTRADICTIONS. Our sinewy sense of practicality and earthiness is juxtaposed against a strain of idealism. Our desire to be detached from Old World machinations is exceeded only by the depths of our emotional involvement with the human commonwealth. The energy we put into public proclamations of virtue is equaled, if not surpassed, by our private expressions of self-doubt. At one and the same time we advertise our excellence and apologize for our achievements. Our benefactions are both proclaimed and deprecated.

There is a persistent quality in the national character that not even the contradictions can obscure. This is our fascination with change. America, perhaps more than any nation in history, was designed to anticipate and accommodate itself to new turnings. Philosophically and temperamentally, the nation has been an instrument of change.

MEN LIKE JEFFERSON AND LINCOLN believed that every great development or change in history begins with advocacy. The change may not come about overnight; it may be stonily resisted. But there is also a natural human response to the essentials of purposeful survival. The individual who speaks to this response will be speaking the most important language on earth. He may not be able by himself to create a consensus, but he can communicate his concern. He can draw encouragement from the knowledge that the great ideas of history were originally dependent on individual advocacy and individual response.

Whether such advocacy gets through to other societies depends not solely on the thickness of the barriers surrounding those societies but on the validity of the ideas behind the advocacy and the carrying power of their genuineness. Some governments may hold back, but an idea directed to world sanity and safety cannot be muted indefinitely.

THE GREATEST TRAGEDY of dictatorship is that the minds of the majority may become so drugged that they may be amenable to barbarism. The danger is not only that we may be caught off guard but that we may slide into dictatorship without being pushed.

THERE IS ALWAYS a wide margin in democracy for cleavages and divergences; indeed, in normal times democracy thrives on them. But there comes a time when the margin must shrink, when differences must be subordinated to common resolution in the face of a common danger. To stray far out beyond the margin; to allow what are really minor differences to become magnified and intensified to the point where more important issues are sidetracked or obscured; to obstruct or impede the national welfare because of petty politics or prejudice—all this is inexplicable treason.

ONE OF OUR DIFFICULTIES is that people at the top in government spend so much time on strategy that almost no time is spent on history. There are so many movers and shakers that there is hardly any room for thinkers.

JEFFERSON'S ADMONITION on the relationship between government and people on critical matters has been quoted so many times that it has become something of a political chestnut. Even so, there is no better way of saying it:

I know of no safe depository of the ultimate powers of society but the people themselves and, if we think them not enlightened enough to exercise their control with a wholesome direction, the remedy is not to take it from them, but to inform their discretion by education.

GOVERNMENTS ARE NOT BUILT to perceive large truths. Only people can perceive great truths. Governments specialize in small and intermediate truths. They have to be instructed by their people in great truths. And the particular truth in which they need instruction today is that new means for meeting the largest problems on earth have to be created. Individual nations can unleash wars but are incapable individually of preventing them.

IT IS DIFFICULT TO KNOW what is worse—a government that ignores the highest aspirations of its people or a government that falsely takes credit for them.

OLD DOGMAS AND IDEOLOGIES are losing their power to inspire or terrify. They are no longer prime sources of intellectual energy and have become instead traditional symbols, objects of generalized attachments and loyalties.

"Something is happening," Teilhard de Chardin wrote, "to the whole structure of human consciousness. A fresh kind of life is starting. In the face of such an upheaval, no one can remain indifferent." The century of Marx and Engels has ended. Marxian doctrine is breaking up, both outside and inside the Soviet Union. The Marxian prophecy about the emergence under capitalism in the United States of a working class with an intense class consciousness has not materialized. Quite the contrary, the working class in the United States insists on seeing itself much more in middle-class terms than in terms of the class struggle. Edward Bellamy has proved to be a far more accurate prophet than Marx, predicting even more fluidity in the social structure than existed a century ago.

THE TROUBLE WITH the proposition that politics is the art of the possible is that so many politicians are inartistic. It takes artistry to deal with the mysteries of human response. It calls for confidence in the magic of human possibility. Winston Churchill didn't spin out homilies about things that couldn't be done, using up valuable time in the process; he created options and pursued them. Pericles and Lincoln didn't content themselves with extolling the dead; they gave the living something to live for. The real leader is both architect and builder, not waiting for structures to materialize but of the blue, but enabling people to see that edifices began with ideas.

IN THE PAST the world didn't merely slough off its primitive ideas or stumble out of them. Not infrequently what would happen is that a few great men were unafraid to appeal directly to the good sense and quality of integrity that are deep within people and that only have to be awakened in order to constitute the strongest force known in history. The capacity of people to respond to that type of leadership may be greater than the nominal leaders think. A generation that is anticipating a rendezvous with destiny deserves and needs to be challenged.

A GOVERNMENT SHOULD BE not just an officialdom but an educational enterprise. "It is not a fossil but a plant," said Emerson.

THE GOVERNMENT CRIES OUT that its secrecy has been violated. Of what stuff does this secrecy consist? Not infrequently it consists of miscalculations, errors of historic proportions and attempts to conceal them, and plans and manipulations that run counter to constitutional government and that reflect contempt for free institutions. The fact that such materials have been classified as "Secret" is understandable in terms of the threat to the personal security of the men who made the errors and did the classifying. But it is not tolerable to the American people, whose security is tied to clearly defined constitutional safeguards.

THE MAIN QUESTION is whether the men at the controls know how to operate the controls. The problem for everyone, regardless of age, is whether we are sensitive enough to know what is happening to our world and whether we are intelligent enough to survive.

WHAT WE HAVE MOST TO FEAR is not the triumph of communism but the default of democracy. The time has come to regard democracy not as a set of abstract notions but as a practical design for living, concerned with food, jobs, schools, and a creative culture.

IT IS DIFFICULT to conceive of any crime by a state—even the oppression or persecution of a minority—which is as great as the crime a majority can inflict on itself by isolating itself from the potentialities of human beings.

DEMOCRACY HAS A TREASURY—a treasury of writings marking the centuries-old struggle of human beings to secure, protect, and enlarge their liberties. These writings show democracy to be no invention or innovation singularly our own but a goal in almost every period in history and in almost every land. America's own literature of liberty is in many ways a reflection—in other ways a culmination—of the crusade for a government that people could call their own.

NO GREATER POLITICAL or philosophical fallacy exists than the notion that freedom is not really an ideology. The ideology of freedom is fused with the nature of human beings. It exists in the molecular structure of natural rights. It is based on the proposition that government exists for the purpose of enhancing and protecting those rights. The rights do not have to be created or contrived. They come with the gift of life. The good society may recognize these rights but it cannot invent them or expunge them. Its obligation is to create the conditions under which they can grow and be secure.

THERE IS A GROWING SENSE of disquiet in the American soul. It involves the relationship of Americans to their own history. It involves their understanding of the national purpose. It involves, finally, their sense of connection with their government. There seems to be a feeling that the country is being steadily separated from the moral base on which so many of its traditions have rested.

A FREE SOCIETY—at least this free society—has certain propositions that have gone into its making. These propositions aren't all political. One of the main propositions that had a certain vitality at the time this particular society was founded was that the individual man has a natural goodness inside him, that he is capable of responding to truth, that he is endowed with the capacity to recognize beauty and be enlarged by it.

A FREE SOCIETY is not just a nation. It is an idea. It is a natural sovereignty committed to the cause of human sovereignty. It is an instrument through which we can work for a fuller life— whether in terms of physical needs or our creative and spiritual reach. This ideology is real and it is ours.

THE GENUINE LIBERAL believes in the consistent and comprehensive improvement of human society, holding to the idea that a human being is a sovereign cause and that the nation exists for the purpose of serving this cause. Liberalism does not expect this concept to be universally accepted or celebrated but believes motion in this direction is where progress begins.

The genuine liberal sees no weakness in accepting the good faith of those who disagree with him. He sees no disgrace in admitting that he may be wrong. He is passionate but not punitive about his position. He has no conditioned reflexes about slogans or labels. Each situation has its own nature and its own requirements.

THE TERM CONSERVATIVE stands for stability as opposed to innovation; for restraint as opposed to daring; for the preservation of inherited conditions as opposed to drastic reform. These ideas are not only compatible with a free society; they have an essential place in it, along with genuine liberalism. True conservatism is opposed to liberalism but not destructive of it. Both conservatism and liberalism serve as the twin structural supports of constitutional government.

Genuine conservatism can be distorted. It can be misused. But the tradition will survive—but not without pain or excitement.

ONE OF THE BASIC PRINCIPLES that has meant much in our history is that not men but laws are supreme in any sane society. The reason is clear. Men have a way of losing their balance. When this happens to good men, the effect can be disquieting. When it happens to bad men, the effect can be disastrous. In either case, government should not be unduly dependent on the ability of men to remain free of error but on the surrounding structure that forces errors into the open.

THE THEORY on which this government was set up was that good government depends less on good men than upon good laws. Indeed, the easiest way for good men to turn bad is to give them a privileged position where their power can be used beyond their own designated functions.

Nuclear bombs are the quintessence of raw power in the

modern world. They call for the severest controls—not only over the bombs themselves, but over the men who have the authority to make them.

THERE IS HOPE in human changeability. This goes beyond the recognition of a divine itch or the sudden notion that there is an extra minute before midnight. Hope today—and it may be the only hope—resides in the world-wide emergence of the articulate and communicating citizen. What he wants and what he does mean more and more to the governments of which he is a part. The American experiment has succeeded in a way that Madison and Hamilton never dared dream it would. Its essential claim—that nothing is more important than man—has been echoed in every continent. The individual man has come into his own. Thinking, feeling, musing, complaining, fending, creating, building, evading, desiring, he has become more important to the operators of his government than ever before. The question, therefore, is not whether man is capable of prolonging and ennobling his stay on earth. The question is whether he recognizes his prime power—and also his duty— for accomplishing that purpose.

THE PRINCIPAL LANGUAGE of the twentieth century must be concerned with the awakening of vast multitudes to the possibilities rather than to the limitations of life. If we have difficulty with that particular vocabulary it is not because of the distance that separates us from those multitudes but because of the distance that separates us from the meaning of America itself.

IF THE THEORY of human perfectibility is rejected, then it may be only a matter of time before we become ground up in the wheels we have sent spinning so furiously. But if human uniqueness is defined as the capacity to conceive that which has never been conceived before, then acceleration can be relieved of its terrors. Our difficulty has never been in doing things; it has been in choosing what to do. The ultimate test is not of skills but of purposes and desires. We have already transformed nature: Are we to say that we are unable to transform ourselves? Is it reasonable to believe that a species that has demonstrated a capacity to lift itself off its planet is unable to raise its sights?

THOMAS JEFFERSON LOOKED FORWARD to a time when all barbarism would disappear from the earth. If he were alive today he would take note of the persistence and extension of barbarism but, as a believer in perfectibility, he would warn against the conclusion that men are essentially barbarous. With Franklin, Emerson, William James, and Holmes, he would resist theories of historical inevitability. He would not be intimidated by the momentum of events into believing that a great reversal could not be brought about. He would also probably try to remind us that no idea figured more largely in the making of American society than that history was what men wanted it to be and that civilization is what happens when men have intelligent desires.

AN AGE WHICH IS DESENSITIZED to evils and horrors is also desensitized to its glories and its opportunities. The essential task, then, is to regenerate the vital responses, to reopen access to the clarifying functions of conscience, and to restore the capacity to dream about a better life. Despite all the billowing evidence to the contrary, humans are still capable of good purposes and decent works. We can still recapture command of our existence and the forces that are shaping it. And this regeneration requires only self-recognition to become real. When enough people can comprehend the reality of the human family, the beginnings of a genuine safety will emerge.

IN THE CENTRIFUGE of the twentieth century, man is whirling away from the center of his own being. The farther out he spins, the more blurred his view of himself, of what he might be, and of his relationship to the nameless faces in the crowd. The separation is not just between body and place; it is between mind and reason.

Ultimately, the acceleration produces irreverence. Men in increasing motion conquer distance but have little ground to stand on. Values take on a free-floating quality. The disconnection makes for distortion and an unfamiliarity that breeds contempt. The main vein of irreverence in our time is nihilistic, brutal, and anti-human. Basically, it is directed against life itself.

ONE OF THE UNHAPPY CHARACTERISTICS of modern man is that he lives in a state of historical disconnection. He has not put his experience to work in coping with new dangers. He has tended to detach himself from the wisdom so slowly and painfully built up over long centuries. He has made the mistake of thinking that because there is so much that is new in the nature of contemporary crises that the past has nothing of value to say to us.

THERE WAS NO PROBLEM, Hegel liked to think, that was not penetrable by thought. This is encouraging enough, but Hegel lived at a time when the problem of scrutinizing living history was not yet battered and confounded by acceleration. Into a few decades have been compressed more change, more thrust, more tossing about of men's souls and gizzards than have been spaced out over most of the human chronicle until then. The metabolism of history has gone berserk.

DESPITE NATIONAL BOUNDARIES and belligerently different ideological systems, the main confrontation in today's world cuts across national boundaries and ideological lines. The ultimate divisions take place within the societies, not between them. On one side are those who comprehend or sense the meaning of the acceleration, who perceive that new connections among men have to be created regardless of their diversity, and who move almost instinctively toward building those universal institutions that can serve the city of man. On the other side are those who think in terms of separatism, the perpetuation of group egos, the manning of tribal battle stations, and the lures of compartmentalization.

If we have learned nothing else, it is that the ideas of the poets and artists penetrate where everything else has failed. The question, therefore, is not as much whether "Everyman" is capable of response, whatever his station, as whether he has something and someone to respond to.

The same acceleration that has produced disarray and irreverence can give man confidence in achieving big goals within the short time it is necessary to achieve them. It can give him confidence, too, in the reach of his intelligence for finding answers of almost infinite complexity. Progress lies not in a rejection of acceleration but in a proper respect for the possibilities of mind.

MUCH OF OUR ACHE AND BROODING are the result of our difficulty in using ourselves fully. We perform compartmentalized tasks in a compartmentalized world. We are reined in—physically, socially, spiritually. Only rarely do we have a sense of fulfilling ourselves through total contact with a total challenge. We find it difficult to make real connections with others. But there are vast surges of conscience, natural purpose, and goodness inside us demanding air and release. And we have our own potentialities, the regions of which are far broader than we can ever guess at—a potential that keeps nagging at us to be fully used.

WE LIVE IN AN AGE remarkable less for its destructiveness than for its desensitization. People have learned how to make their accommodations with the irrational. The missiles and the megatons have been metabolized into everyday facts of life. What is happening today is that the natural reactions of the individual against violence are being blunted. The individual is being desensitized by living history. We are developing new reflexes and new responses that tend to slow down the moral imagination and relieve us of essential indignation over impersonal hurt. We are becoming casual about brutality. We have made our peace with violence.

The desensitization of twentieth-century man is more than a danger to the common safety. It represents the loss or impairment of the noblest faculties of human life—the ability to share sorrow and create hope; the ability to think and respond beyond one's wants. There are some things we have no right ever to get used to. One of these most certainly is brutality. The other is irrationality. Both brutality and irrationality have now come together and are moving toward a dominant pattern. If the pattern is to be resisted and changed, a special effort must be made. A very special effort.

THE SUSPICION GROWS that the direct need that exists between humans is deeply felt but not fully exercised. We are becoming masters of the impersonal and inanimate. Our energy and even our emotions are going into things; the things serve us but they come between us, changing the relationship of person to person. And the things take on an authority that we accept without protest. Impersonality is epidemic. It is almost as though we fear direct contact, almost as though the soul of man has become septic.

WE LIVE AT A TIME when people seem afraid to be themselves, when they seem to prefer a hard, shiny exterior to the genuineness of deeply felt emotion. Sophistication is prized and sentiment is dreaded. It is made to appear that one of the worst blights on a reputation is to be called a do-gooder. The literature of the day is remarkably devoid of themes on the natural goodness of man, seeing no dramatic power in the most powerful fact of the human mixture. The values of the time lean toward a phony toughness, casual violence, and cheap emotion, yet we are shocked when youngsters confess to have tortured and killed because they enjoyed it and because they thought it was the thing to do.

IN THE TWENTIETH CENTURY man has no escape from man. And the human confrontation will continue until surh time as man defaults or creates the means for safeguarding life. The choice today is not between escape and disaster. It is, as it always was, between the satisfactions that blind and the obligations that awaken.

NEVER BEFORE has so much leisure time been available to so many. Leisure hours now exceed working hours. But we have a genius for cluttering. We have somehow managed to persuade ourselves that we are too busy to think, too busy to read, too busy to look back, too busy to look ahead, too busy to understand that all our wealth and all our power are not enough to safeguard our future unless there is also a real understanding of how we can meet the very real dangers that confront us.

THE PAST sets up far fewer barriers to the understanding of causes and effects than does the present. You assemble your reference materials about the past; there they rest, accessible and obedient, waiting to be sorted out and judged. But the facts of the present won't sit still for a portrait; they are constantly vibrating, full of clutter and confusion. "History," said Lamartine, "teaches us everything—even the future."

THE CASH LOST EACH YEAR in the United States amounts to about seventy-five dollars per capita—money that has fallen out of pockets, is misplaced, and so forth. The total average income for most of the human occupants of this planet comes to about sixty-nine dollars per person. The average American thus loses more money each year than almost anyone else earns.

There is something damnably itchy about these statistics. We feel like scratching but don't quite know where to find the bite. What do we do about unwanted distinctions? Do we celebrate the discovery that we have the biggest garbage removal bill in town? Do we congratulate ourselves on the fact that the drip from our leaky faucet in one day represents more water than the average Asian family in a drought-stricken area will drink or use in a month?

Whatever one does or does not do about these jabbing statistics, one thing at least is clear. They don't lend themselves to adjustment. No philosophical formulation, be it ever so sophisticated, can possibly provide the accommodating ointment. The notion that we have to take the world as it is doesn't quite relieve the itch. What do we do? Perhaps we had better go on scratching—at least until we find the bite.

THE ESSENTIAL PROBLEM in a computerized age remains the same as it has always been. That problem is not solely how to be more productive, more comfortable, more content, but how to be more sensitive, more sensible, more proportionate, more alive. The computer makes possible a phenomenal leap in human proficiency; it demolishes the fences around the practical and even the theoretical intelligence. But the question persists and indeed grows whether the computer will make it easier or harder for human beings to know who they really are, to identify their real problems, to respond more fully to beauty, to place adequate value on life, and to make their world safer than it now is.

ELECTRONIC BRAINS can reduce the profusion of dead ends involved in research. But they can't eliminate the foolishness and decay that come from the unexamined life. Nor do they connect us to the things we have to be connected to—the reality of pain in others, the possibilities of creative growth in ourselves, the memory of the race, and the rights of the next generation.

THERE IS A TENDENCY to mistake data for wisdom, just as there has always been a tendency to confuse logic with values, intelligence with insight. Unobstructed access to facts can produce unlimited good only if it is matched by the desire and ability to find out what they mean and where they lead. Facts are terrible things if left sprawling and unattended. They are too easily regarded as evaluated certainties rather than as the rawest of raw materials crying to be processed into the texture of logic. It requires a very unusual mind, Whitehead said, to undertake the analysis of a fact. The computer can provide a correct number, but it may be an irrelevant number until judgment is pronounced.

HUMAN BEINGS in a world of computerized intelligence are taking on a quality of spindled artifacts; they are losing their faces. They are also losing their secrets. Their mistakes and indiscretions are metabolized by a data base, never to be forgotten. Nothing is more universal than human fallibility; nothing is more essential than forgiveness or absolution. Yet statistical maintenance is as remorseless as it is free of redeeming judgments nourished by intangibles or the passing of time.

WE HAVE EXALTED CHANGE in everything but ourselves. We have leaped centuries ahead in inventing a new world to live in, but we know little or nothing about the conditions of life. We have surrounded and confounded ourselves with gaps—gaps between revolutionary science and evolutionary anthropology, between cosmic gadgets and human wisdom, between intellect and conscience. The struggle between science and morals that Henry Thomas Bucke foresaw more than a century ago has been all but won by science. Given time, we might be expected to bridge those gaps normally; but by our own hand, we are destroying even time. Whatever bridges we have to build and cross, we will have to do so in our own self-shortened time.

WHAT IS MOST CHARACTERISTIC of "modern" man is not his ready power but his ultimate powerlessness, not his ability to mobilize vast force but his inability to protect himself against it.

SEQUENTIAL THOUGHT is the most difficult in the entire range of human effort. It is the result of systematic training. Yet speed is being valued out of all proportion to its usefulness. Johnny is expected to read faster, study faster, write faster, and think faster. This is less the fault of his teachers than of the world itself. But the problems posed by an Age of Speed are not met by snap judgments. We meet our problems only as we comprehend them and give them sustained and sequential thought. The quickest way to compound these problems is to put them in a pressure cooker.

Some vignettes of leaders and people of stature I had the privilege of meeting in the course of my work. (My ventures in the political arena ended in 1978, which accounts for the absence of more recent names.)

———

WINSTON CHURCHILL ENABLED MILLIONS of people to discover their capacity for total response. He taught them that it was far less painful to pit the whole of themselves against a monstrous force than it was to sit on the sidelines half alive. The beginning of the end of the Hitlerian nightmare came not when the Nazi military juggernaut was slowed down but much earlier, largely because of Churchill. When free men became unblocked, when they stopped equivocating about values, when they put aside relativistic notions of good and evil, and when they came to respect the rights of generations yet unborn. Because of his greatness, they lost what they most needed losing—their cynicism and feelings of tentativeness and panic in the face of national and personal danger. It was not Churchill's rhetoric alone that enabled them to do this. It was the recognition Churchill gave them that history was what men made it.

Courage to Churchill was more than a spirited charge into a hurricane of flying bullets. It was a wondrous human assortment—hearty laughter, warm feelings, and the enjoyment of living in general. The highest privilege was the freedom to choose; the meanest affliction was to live without options. He gave options to a world quickly running out of time and space. He offered evidence that human beings are not at the mercy of historical determinism, that they do not have to accept helplessness. He did much more than to sound the call to action. He shattered the notion of a philosophical or political inevitability. In so doing he gave reality to freedom and nobility to reality.

THE FIRST TIME I SAW F.D.R. was in October 1937 at a press conference in the White House. The room was tightly packed with newsmen, and I prowled around the edge of the crowd, trying to get a full view of the man sitting behind the desk. Finally, at the left side of the room, I was able to find a vantage point that gave me a full, clear view of the President. I will never forget him as I saw him then. He was tanned, robust, electric with life. I remember thinking that I had never seen a healthier looking human being. There was also the look of greatness. It was inevitable. Anyone who could come back out of retirement after having been afflicted with a dreadful disease that shrank his limbs and that made it impossible for him to walk unaided would be great for that reason alone. You could see his braces where they entered his shoes, huge pieces of steel that seemed to reach inside you as well. It did things to you because one hundred and thirty million people were leaning on this man and the weight, if anything, was making him stronger and bigger.

Anyone who doesn't remember the Depression years, the

Hitlerian horrors, and the ordeal of World War II, especially in the early period, cannot comprehend the sense of dependence on this man, or the way millions of people trusted him. To the people who loved him—and this meant most Americans—he was everything a leader should be: strong, open, honest, unflappable, daring, lucky, gregarious, noble, joyous, eloquent, zesty, accessible. F.D.R. was a winner in an age up to its ears in losers.

A SOCIETY BECOMES EXPLOSIVE when the poor feel they have no friends in high places. Eleanor Roosevelt filled the role of personal friend for millions of Americans who needed an outlet for their hurts. She couldn't reshape society; she couldn't eradicate the squalor; she couldn't change the color of people's skins. But she was able to exert vast influence inside the government. She was never oblivious of the power that went with being the wife of the President. The heads of government departments could expect a weekly barrage from Mrs. Roosevelt, asking them to look into this or that special situation, or to take this or that initiative. She must have received at least a thousand letters a week—an expectant mother who didn't know where to go for the birth of her baby; a coal miner who had a bad heart but who couldn't afford to stop working; a black professor who had an idea for establishing a recreational center for small children of needy families; and so on, endlessly. Not a single request went unanswered. Not always did the applicants get exactly the kind of help they sought, but no one had the feeling he or she was ignored. Most of all, everyone knew she cared. She was the national conscience and gave character to the entire society. People—unfeeling, unthinking people—sometimes made jokes about her looks. She gave cartoonists an easy time: large, protruding teeth, oversized mouth, sloping chin. But everyone who knew her—everyone who saw her—knew they had never seen a more beautiful human being. From her I learned a great deal about the power of human graciousness and compassion.

HARRY S. TRUMAN'S FAVORITE POEM was Tennyson's *Locksley Hall* with its vision of a world society at peace under a Parliament of

Man. He kept the poem in his wallet. He showed it to me once when I asked about his dream for America. But there was an inconsistency between the message in the poem and his decision to drop the world's first atomic bomb on human beings. That decision was more closely connected to the beginning of a world nuclear arms race than to the beginning of a world parliament. The bomb to Truman was a powerful new weapon, one he thought it would be irresponsible not to use if the war could be shortened by even a single day. But for many of the scientists who produced the bomb, it was far more than a weapon; it was the start of an entirely new period in human history in which only the control of force, and not its use, could provide even minimal assurances of human survival. At the very least, they felt an ultimatum should be issued to Japan, on the basis of a demonstration bombing under international auspices. Truman rejected their urging; to the end he defended the decison to drop the bomb in the manner he did. No one doubts his gutsiness or his firmness; whether these particular qualities were what was most needed is something future generations will have to decide.

NO ONE GAVE BETTER REASONS for not electing a military man to the Presidency than General Dwight D. Eisenhower himself three months before his nomination. The kind of training a professional soldier receives, he said, runs directly counter to what is required in the Presidency. The emphasis of the military is on authority and obedience; the emphasis in public office is on communication and consent. But he accepted the nomination and won, whereupon he set out to prove he not only would not abuse power, he would be very reluctant to exercise it. He created large franchises in the government: The foreign policy franchise he turned over to John Foster Dulles; the domestic policy franchise to Sherman Adams. He later said he thought Dulles was too addicted to the plot-and-counterplot approach to foreign policy, was too convoluted, too manipulative. He thought Adams was open and congenial enough but didn't inspire confidence. After Adams returned to New Hampshire and John Foster Dulles died, Eisenhower was forced to become his own President and surprised himself by liking the job. But he was never able to crack through the concrete blocks of bureaucracy, nor was he able to rise above the competing pressures exerted on the President by the Congress, the military, and public opinion. Two weeks before the end of his term he told me that he was looking forward to his freedom—he could hardly wait to devote himself to the cause of peace. As ex-President he could have unobstructed access to his fellow citizens. Significantly, the first thing he did on leaving office was to warn the nation against the increasing strength of the military and industrial complex. He had demonstrated beyond question in the White House that he was a citizen even before he was a general, but he had barely begun to exercise the office himself when his term expired. He was a man of infinite good will but he was more a regent than a President.

ADLAI STEVENSON HAD ALL THE QUALITIES that went with leadership—intelligence, energy, compassion, integrity, eloquence, charm—yet he was the last in any company to see himself in a leadership role. He loved to analyze problems but didn't want to arrogate to himself the job to go charging off after solutions. He held high positions—as Governor of Illinois and United States Ambassador to the United Nations—but his abilities were so vast that there was hardly a time when he wasn't living far under his capacities. Abraham Lincoln, of all the people in American history, held the highest claim on his moral imagination. Most Americans idolize Lincoln because of what they consider to be his ability to make great decisions; what fascinated Stevenson about Lincoln was Lincoln's agony in facing up to those decisions. Life, especially life at the top, is not simple; and Lincoln to Stevenson was heroic because he recognized complexity, hovered over it, suffered from it, and grew through it. Stevenson bemoaned his lack of time to think and study and read. He sought the company of those who somehow managed to stay on top of expanding knowledge and who, in Socrates's phrase, shunned the unexamined life. But he was also prone to derail your train of thought when you became too serious. A good anecdote to him was one of life's great prizes. He was a marvelous companion but was never lonelier than when in a crowd. He had to be pushed into the public arena yet was often the last to leave. His greatest achievement was that he converted a presidential election campaign into a national classroom. The fact that he was able to analyze issues before an audience of millions seemed to him to be the greatest privilege of his lifetime. All his friends thought he would have made a great President. They were able to persuade millions of Americans of that view; they never quite persuaded the majority or Stevenson himself. The job he really wanted, he told me, was Secretary of State.

HUBERT H. HUMPHREY SAW A HUMAN DIMENSION in the people on whom Sinclair Lewis had laid a curse that went by the name of Babbitt. Hubert could no more deride people than he could avoid returning a smile or accepting an outstretched hand. He would have been the perfect leading character for any play by Oscar Hammerstein; he was in love with the whole human race, and especially that portion of it that lived in the United States.

His father's drugstore, which he described as a profound educational experience, could have been a backdrop for a movie version of *Main Street.* People came there not just to get relief from their bunions but to engage in the social life of the community. Hubert loved the drugstore, loved everything about it—the rock candy over which the youngsters would hover with their pennies; the half-empty bottles of cough medicine that people would return for partial refunds when they recovered from their colds; the emergency telephone calls to his father's house in the middle of the night when people couldn't reach their doctors; the hurried trips to the store at 3:00 A.M. in response to calls from the doctors themselves; being big brother and father-confessor to the kids in the neighborhood. It was only a matter of time, his friends believed, before Hubert would become President of the United States. That time never came; Vietnam came first. What I learned from him most of all is that honest sentiment, honest exuberance, honest ambition are a powerful force in personal relationships but may have their penalties in public.

NIKITA KHRUSHCHEV. Squat, powerful, volatile, personable, compelling, direct, unambiguous. In private conversation, he was far more deferential, more reserved, than he had been pictured in the news accounts. He listened intently, did not interrupt. He wore silk shirts and gold cuff links. His winter underwear showed through the slits of his shirt cuffs. He was very frank in saying that he had difficulty at times in fitting into the ideology to which he had made a commitment and which he was trying to change. He believed that Josef Stalin had disfigured Soviet history and that public habits of acquiescence, hero-worship, and immobility under Stalin were enfeebling the nation. He tried to liberate the people from their Stalinist past, just as he tried to de-dogmatize the ideology. He was a total realist who understood the limits of ideological and national forces in a nuclear age. He would not forego pressing for any advantages for his nation, but he would not allow considerations of national pride or ego to push him over the nuclear cliff. He had an underlying admiration for the United States and its history and believed that the logic of history dictated a good working relationship between the Soviet Union and the United States. To him, nationalism was more important than ideology. History and geography combined to juxtapose the Soviet Union against the People's Republic of China. He succeeded in winning the governing council of the Soviet Communist Party to an acceptance of these realities but he failed to gain support for himself personally. Yet his unceremonious ouster as Prime Minister was in itself a vindication of his essential purpose, which was to provide for succession without upheaval. The force of his personality inside the Communist world may have had a far greater impact on history than any theories of inevitable forces or historical determinism. History is still primarily what men make it.

JOHN F. KENNEDY IMMERSED HIMSELF in history long before he made it. When he moved to the White House he didn't superimpose himself upon American history; he fitted into it just as it fitted into him. He didn't have to wander through government archives looking for records of ideas and acts that had gone into the making of the American purpose. This knowledge was part of him and he put it to work. "The laws," wrote DeTocqueville, "allow a President to be strong but circumstances keep him weak." To function well in such a setting, a man must love his job or have a superhuman disposition. John Kennedy had both. Few tried harder to comprehend all the implications of the decisions they had to make. He rarely left a sentence or a situation uncompleted. Always there was the effort to state a problem in reasonable terms in a way that might appeal to reasonable men. He would have had no trouble in qualifying for inclusion in the kind of company Carl Becker wrote about some years ago in a striking book called *The Heavenly City of the Eighteenth Century Philosophers*. The men who founded the United States were men of reason who believed that a good government was distinguished from bad to the extent that it could develop a memory and put it to work. Their "heavenly city" was a state of enlightenment in which human intelligence and rational thought could foster the perfectibility of man and human society in general. The key to John F. Kennedy, therefore, was that he was in the American rationalist tradition. Not every problem had an answer but every problem had its origins and component parts, each of which called for weighing and grading, and all of which were related to one another in a way that increased the probability of a workable answer. Most of all, he enabled brave and reasonable men to come out of hiding. He taught the American people to respect youth and to cry over it.

My most vivid memory of J. F. K. was of him striding through the White House gardens, a tall, lithe young man on his way to his office after playing with his children. A staff meeting had ended earlier than usual and he had joyously seized the new-found time to romp with the youngsters. Still striding, he discussed Khrushchev with me, then abruptly changed the subject and said that he was due to give a speech in fifteen minutes to music honor students on the White House lawn. He hadn't even thought about his talk. Would I prepare some notes for him? He had to speak for ten minutes or so. I looked at him in disbelief. Fifteen minutes to prepare a ten minute talk. I said I would do my best. He sat me down at a typewriter in an anteroom off the Oval Office. It seemed to me that the president might use the occasion to refute the notion that America was a cultural wasteland. Evidence: more people went to concerts in the previous twelve months than to baseball games; sales of books had topped thirty million a month; America ballet companies and symphony orchestras were enjoying unprecedented popularity abroad. Typing as rapidly as I could on library catalogue cards, I completed the assignment in twelve minutes, then went downstairs to the White House dining room. A few minutes later, Larry O'Brien came by and sat down. "Now I've seen it all," he said. "The president had four or five minutes before he was due to speak to the music students, so he sprinted down to the White House swimming pool, ripped off his clothes, and dove in, swimming with one arm and using his other arm to hold the text of the talk he was going to give—which he was reading for the first time." The young President had to take life on the run. Everything went very fast. He was lost to the American people and to the world even before he had served out his first term.

THE MOST VIVID and perhaps most disturbing memory I have of Lyndon Johnson is standing behind him in the White House while he spoke to the Presidential Scholars in 1964. An electronic prompter flashed the text of his talk on a glass screen atop the lectern; it was invisible to the audience. A line came up on the prompter: "We can defeat the Communists in North Vietnam without sending American troops." The President stared at the prompter and said nothing, then reached for a glass of water. He let the line pass unspoken, then went on with his speech. I left Washington that night with a terrible foreboding. Three months later American troops in large numbers were engaged in battle in Vietnam.

He gave dramatic expression to the strengths and weaknesses that are inherent in the American presidency. It was his misfortune that the particular challenge of his presidency called for someone who could rise above the conflicting pressures rather than someone who could be adroit at balancing them. The Vietnam War produced more pressure than even the politically skilled Johnson could handle. There were those inside the government who believed in the limited war concept. There were those who urged him to go all the way. There were those who urged a full pullout. Lyndon Johnson's training had been as a compromiser, but the contending forces here admitted no compromise. He had to choose or create a new choice—and this was where he was wanting. As a politician, he liked to believe that time was always on his side. But time in Vietnam worked against him. The President's problem—and America's tragedy—was that even deferral or delay could only lead to a pyramiding of the original miscalculations. He never really understood the extent to which nationalism could transcend ideology. He viewed communism as a unified and monolithic force; he was surprised to discover that the historical, regional, and national issues completely obliterated the notion of ideological sway. Johnson, who grew up politically under FDR and who, perhaps more than any other political figure of his time, had the political skills and social vision to create a latter-day New Deal, had to settle for a lesser role in history than his capabilities promised. Vietnam was more than a political dilemma, It was an arena filled with human casualties, Vietnamese and American. Lyndon Baines Johnson was an accomplished political craftsman at a time when only a towering moral figure could have carried the day.

GERALD FORD TURNED OUT TO BE a lot better than his intellectual detractors thought possible. He grew up as a hard-line critic of liberal Democratic presidents, but the realities of the presidency caused him to reject the advice of his old companions and to identify himself with middle-of-the-roaders. As ex-President, he initially withheld support from Ronald Reagan because he thought Reagan was too far to the right—and at odds with what he believed was a new tradition of moderation within his party. He was "appointed" to the Presidency by Richard M. Nixon after the worst political scandal in the nation's history. But his prompt pardon of his predecessor, blocking any legal resolution of all the points at issue, probably cost Ford reelection and an opportunity to demonstrate that he was far more of a national unifier, and far more of a constructive force in the nation's foreign policy, than his critics ever dreamt possible.

THERE WAS MUCH about Albert Einstein that called for attention—his casual way of dressing, with the inevitable sweater-shirt, the slacks, and the sandals—but always I found myself drawn back to the large, probing eyes. When he talked, he gave you the impression that you were at the center of the universe. His concentration on you was not of the intense, penetrating type that made you feel he was scrutinizing you and probing for hidden meanings. It was the concentration of a man who was listening to you carefully and sympathetically and was encouraging you to speak your piece.

He lived in Princeton, New Jersey, in a small white frame house on Mercer Street, not far from the university. The house was a striking extension of the man—restrained, comfortable, mellow. A narrow flight of stairs led to his book-lined study. A large picture window looked out on a modest garden. He had no hesitation in answering the usual question put to him by friends and visitors: Did he regret his role in the development of the world's first atomic bomb? He said he had no apologies to make for urging the United States to undertake nuclear research as a defense against Germany, but he regretted the decision to use the bomb without warning. The decision to drop not just one bomb but two was one that he himself couldn't understand and that he profoundly regretted—not just as a scientist who figured in the original sequence of events leading to the making of the bomb, but as a human being who was concerned about the American legacy to the future. Peace to him was more than a commitment; it was an obsession.

His name commands universal respect, even awe. The world's people may not comprehend his theory of relativity, or exactly why $E = mc^2$ unlocked so many cosmic secrets, but they have an instinctive sense that Albert Einstein dealt not just in scientific truths but in moral truths. Out of his brain came a design for living in an atomic age that, if sufficiently understood and pursued may yet lead to sanity and safety on this earth.

The finest evaluation of Einstein's place in history came from Jawaharlal Nehru. The date was April 18, 1955. The place was Bandung, Indonesia, where the newly independent nations of Asia and Africa had come together to celebrate their independence. At the morning plenary session, one of the news correspondents handed me a wire saying that Albert Einstein had just died. I passed the cable along to Nehru. He looked at the message, and sat quietly for a few minutes with his hands buried in his face. Then he wrote out a note:

The wisest and greatest man among us has passed away. Not for many years will we fully appreciate that wisdom and greatness. But he has tried to show us the way. Those who have the responsibility for leading nations have a tendency to think only of their own societies. But Albert Einstein has been telling us that we can no longer live in separate worlds. It is that concept of a unified world which all of us—leaders and citizens—must now create and serve.

THE FIRST THING POPE JOHN XXIII SAID when I came into his study was: "Please don't kneel. It's all right. Here, take my hand. I'm nothing very special. I breathe the way everyone else does. It's not hard; I have a large nose, a very large nose." He had no difficulty in reaching out. He didn't believe that God penalizes anyone for not being a Catholic. Religion to him was a matter of individual conscience. Nonbelievers who had audiences with Pope John XXIII were told that he included them in his prayers. He believed that the world's peoples had to make distinctions between old realities that led to a dead end, and new realities that could lead to a creative and safe existence for the human community. His historic encyclical letter "Peace on Earth" was in the nature of a declaration of interdependence for the human species. Beyond the stress and clamor of nationalities there must be created a viable new form of world organization with authority to regulate the dealings among nations under justice and law. In its analysis of the human condition of man; in its assertion of freedom of conscience in religious and political matters; in its discussion of the dangers of a runaway nuclear arms race; in its comprehension of the nature of nuclear war; in its call for a strengthened United Nations under law and responsive to the needs of the world community—in all these respects, the encyclical letter had historic proportions. It was at once eloquent and practical, diagnostic and therapeutic, historical and contemporary. Most important of all, it set men's minds in a new direction, enabling them to break loose from notions of inevitability, defeatism, and despair.

In *Mont Saint-Michel and Chartres*, Henry Adams wrote that

"Under any conceivable system the process of getting God and man under the same roof—of bringing two independent energies under the same control" has been an extraordinarily difficult and painful process. Pope John had this kind of architecture in mind. We live in an age which looks to physical motion for its spectacular achievements. A man encased in a metallic capsule spinning through outer space; the heart of an atom pried open and releasing vast stores of energy; streams of electrons flashing images of something happening thousands of miles away—these are the main articles of wonder in the modern world. But they did not have the impress on history of an eighty-one-year-old man dying of cancer, using the papacy to make not just his own church but all churches fully relevant and fully useful in the cause of human unity and peace. The peace sought by Pope John XXIII need not be unattainable once belief in ideas is put ahead of belief in moving parts.

DURING THE 1930s, when Mahatma Gandhi's world influence was strongest, he was an implausible figure to many Americans. He seemed to be the quintessential opposite of the traditional American hero. The qualities most characteristic of the men who built the United States were dynamism, robustness, and venturesomeness. But there is an aspect of the American character that runs just as deep as the traditional respect for boldness and physical strength. Philosophers, writers, and teachers, like Benjamin Franklin, Henry David Thoreau, Ralph Waldo Emerson, Oliver Wendell Holmes, William James, Horace Mann, and John Dewey, occupy high places in American history. These men regarded themselves as world citizens caught up in a great adventure of ideas. Mahatma Gandhi felt himself drawn to men of this stamp and dimension. He acknowledged his philosophical debt to Thoreau's ideas on civil disobedience. He represented dramatic proof that the individual need not be helpless against massed power—that he need not be overwhelmed by any supposed inexorability or fatalism, that there was scope for free will and conviction in the shaping of society, that history could be fluid, not fixed, if people were able to see themselves as global rather than tribal creatures. I saw him only once; he was courteous and enigmatic. When asked about the lessons of his life, what he said is substantially the same as what he said to Nehru: "You will make many journeys. Always keep your destination in mind or you may never get there."

JAWAHARLAL NEHRU LIKED TO WRITE even more than he liked to rule; he felt incomplete when he was unable to assemble his thoughts and commit them to paper. He regarded writing as the most demanding, the most exhausting, but also the most satisfying of the creative arts. Being able to give life to a concept through words; using language as a vehicle of persuasion or as a voyage of intellectual exploration and discovery—all these were vital elements of his philosophy. At times he could write like the most detached and aseptic historian. At other times he would write with extreme sensitivity and grace. In describing a natural setting, he could be all poet. "The Ganges," he wrote, "reminds me of the snow-covered peaks and the deep valleys of the Himalayas . . . Smiling and dancing in the morning sunlight, and dark and gloomy and full of mystery as evening shadows fall; a narrow, slow, and graceful stream in winter, and a vast, roaring thing during monsoon, broad-bosomed almost as the sea, and with something of the sea's power to destroy, the Ganges has been to me a symbol and a memory of the past of India, running into the present, and flowing on to the great ocean of the future."

For many years his writing, quite literally, kept him from losing his mind. This was during his various imprisonments as an agitator for Indian freedom. No one knows how many hundreds of thousands or millions of words he wrote while in jail. His autobiography came out of prison. Few writers before or since have fused in one person more thoroughly the complex essence of East and West. He was a fascinating amalgam of cultures; his formal education was English but his traditions were Indian. His intellect was rooted in the Enlightenment, his spirit in the Vedas. He was avowedly rationalist, but his feelings about India and her people bordered on the spiritual. From him I learned something about the loneliness of men in high station—especially when they desired nothing so much as being able to think, read, and write.

U THANT HAD TO DEAL WITH false and stubborn notions about national security. He had to keep nations from colliding even though they were on a collision course. He was not embittered. Despite all reversals and difficulties, he retained a rock-like belief in the future of the United Nations. He knew there was nothing else on which the future of the human community could be built—nothing else that gave greater promise of protecting human beings from the holocaust-producing weapons in the hands of the national sovereignties. He was a man of limitless good faith and good will. He had incredible qualities of patience and personal serenity. He came from the East but his intellectual horizons were in the West. The most powerful arguments for him to remain at his post came not from officialdom but from everyday people all over the world. Letters arrived by the thousands from people who understood his purposes. He had a constituency of common folk; they made him a custodian of their hopes. He stayed on at his post not just because he had the support of national governments but because of the manifest public support for his own ideas about the future of the United Nations. From him I learned a great deal about the importance of genuine good will in seeking solutions to complicated international problems—or any problems, for that matter.

DOUGLAS MACARTHUR SYMBOLIZED all the notions that went with military heroes, but, emphatic public impressions to the contrary, he was not a militarist. He was not a lover of bombs or a brandisher of swords. He was not fitted to a white horse. Yes—there was grandeur to the man. He could be hard, haughty, impatient. He could drive forward when he had an objective to reach, and he was disdainful of obstructions. And no one surpassed his genius for invoking patriotism. But he was not a tub-thumping jingoist who contrived to juxtapose the national cause against the human cause. "Could I have but one line a century hence crediting me with a contribution to the advance of peace," he once said, "I would gladly yield every honor which has been accorded me in war." Both his supporters and his critics reacted to the military posture, to the rakish tilt of the

cap, to the mystique of the man. And both groups have failed
to see beyond the cluster of medals to the man whose greatest
pride in his career was connected to his land reform program
in Japan and to the clause in the new Japanese constitution out-
lawing war and the means of war. He appeared before an
American Legion convention after the end of the Second
World War and surprised all his listeners by calling for world
government as the best means for preserving the peace. I
learned from him that men come to life in their paradoxes.

ALBERT SCHWEITZER HELPED make it possible for twentieth-century human beings to unlock their moral vision. There is a tendency in a relativistic age to pursue all sides of a question as an
end in itself, thus freeing people of the fatigue of separating
good from evil. The result is a clogging of the moral senses, a
certain feeling of self-consciousness or even discomfort when
questions with ethical content are raised. Schweitzer furnished
evidence that nothing is more natural in life than a moral
response—a moral response that exists independently of precise definition, its use leading not to exhaustion but to new
energy.

The greatness of Schweitzer—indeed the essence of
Schweitzer—was both tangible and symbolic. More important
than what he did for others was what others have done because
of him. At least a half-dozen hospitals in impoverished, remote
areas were established by others in his name. Wherever the
Schweitzer story was known, lives were changed. His main
achievement was a simple one. He was willing to make the ultimate sacrifice for a moral principle. Like Gandhi's, the power
of his appeal was in renunciation. Because he was able to feel a
supreme identification with other human beings he exerted a
greater force than armed men on the march. It is unimportant
whether we call Schweitzer a great religious figure or a great
moral figure or a great philosopher. It suffices that his words
and works are known and that he is loved and has influence
because he enabled men to discover mercy in themselves. The
proof of his genuineness and his integrity is to be found in the
response he awakened in people. He reached countless millions
who never saw him but who were able to identify themselves

with him because of the invisible and splendid fact of his own identification with them. The most important lesson he had learned, he told me, was that the most magnificent cathedrals are not outside you but inside you.

THE EXPRESSIVENESS OF PABLO CASALS'S FEATURES had the dramatic power of a full Ibsen cast. When something engaged his compassion, his face was a tableau. I visited him for the first time at his seaside villa outside San Juan, Puerto Rico, in 1958. Like his friend, Albert Schweitzer, Casals believed that Bach was the greatest of all composers. "But we like Bach for different reasons," he said. "Schweitzer sees Bach in complex architectural terms and acclaims him a master who reigns supreme over the diverse realm of music. I see Bach as a romantic. His music stirs me, helps me to feel fully alive."

His favorite single composition, however, was Brahms's *B Flat Quartet*. From the wall, he took a framed original manuscript, given to him by a Viennese collector, Wilhelm Kuchs. From the first time he had played the *Quartet*, he felt that it was his, that it had some claim upon him. He turned from music to the subject of world peace. The feeling of individual helplessness, he said, was a great and growing problem. But there was an answer. "It is not very complicated. Each person has inside him a basic decency and goodness. If he listens to it and acts on it, he is giving a great deal of what it is the world most needs. But it takes courage."

I visited Casals again when he was eighty-seven. He spoke of being profoundly jolted by terrible events during his life. But never had any tragedy brought him as much sadness as had the assassination of President John F. Kennedy—a leader whom Casals felt was using his great office to try to make a better world and for whom he had performed at the White House in one of his rare appearances as a soloist. Delicately built and frail, Pablo Casals was a giant among men in spirit and creative stature. He saw no disconnection between the arts of man and human institutions.

MARTIN BUBER HAS HAD an extraordinary influence on diverse cultures and philosophies during the mid-twentieth century.

His most popular work, *I and Thou*, penetrated the worlds of psychology, psychiatry, philosophy, and theology, heightening our understanding of the social character of human selfhood. Buber believed that the most acute symptom of the pathology of his time was the inability of peoples to carry on authentic dialogue with one another—a dialogue that would "heed, affirm, and confirm" the existence of another, even when opposing positions were involved. Nothing so much characterizes his contribution to peace through understanding as his own words: "Those who build the great unknown front across mankind shall make it known by speaking unreservedly with one another, not overlooking what divides them but determined to bear this division in common." He did not believe that the world's statesmen and political leaders could be counted on to define the problem and then meet it. They are so involved in the give-and-take of national rivalries that the larger question of human destiny is overlooked. There is one hope, Professor Buber observed. It is for people to become aware. Nothing can be done without awareness. With it, anything is possible. If people know and think and feel, they can talk and act and give leadership to their leaders. The human mind must be used as it was meant to be used—in the cause of human growth and integrity. His life and thought represent a legacy to the future.

FEW MEMORIES ARE MORE VIVID in my mind than walking into Helen Keller's study in total darkness and, suddenly, having Miss Thomson snap on the lights. Helen Keller had been sitting in the blackness for several hours, reading in Braille and working on her correspondence. Only the vibrations in the floor set off by our approach signalled to her our presence. She rose and walked towards us, extending her arms. It was the first time I had met her, and she reached for my head. Very delicately, very slowly, her fingers explored my face and I felt that my innermost being was being examined. The fingers ran lightly over my forehead, eyes, planes of my face, mouth, chin, and neck. There was nothing intrusive about the experience; she made it feel as though it was as natural and unexceptional as a handshake. When we went to her table for dinner, she stopped when she smelled the freshly lit candles, and exclaimed how much she loved to have candles at dinner time. Miss Thomson sat next to her and translated by working her fingers in the palm of Helen Keller's hand in the language they had worked out so beautifully together. We talked about world affairs and music and mutual friends. After dinner she asked me to play the piano and she listened by placing her fingers on the side of the instrument. Her face was open, expectant, luminous. She was one of the finest teachers the human race has produced. She taught us that the human spirit is life-giving, dimensionless, omnipresent. She taught us that the smallest fractions can open out into a great whole. I have never known a more gracious, noble, or lovable human being.

VED MEHTA NEVER REGARDED HIMSELF as a blind person. He has no sight but he travels around the world on his own without a cane or seeing-eye dog or guide. In New York City, where he lives and works (at *The New Yorker* magazine), he goes from home to office or wherever he has to go—crossing streets, entering and leaving buildings, taking elevators, riding subways or busses—on his own. When as a young teenager he would come out to visit us in Connecticut, he would ride the girls' bicycles in the driveway. All his other senses are so highly and exquisitely developed that his brain is like a radar machine, making images out of sounds or the minutest changes of temperature on his skin or the movement of air. In this way, he walks around objects, is able to "see" doorways or curbs or stairways. The only request he makes of his friends is that they not hold his arm to guide him or refer to him as blind. He can identify people by their handshake or their footsteps. These refined perceptions carry over to the world of ideas and events. He has become one of the finest essayists and reporters in contemporary journalism. His understanding of people is no less profound or sensitive than his understanding of society. No one I ever knew provided more eloquent evidence of the possibilities of human development.

ONE OF THE MOST DYNAMIC, restless, original, quixotic, probing minds of the twentieth century belonged to Leo Szilard, the

Hungarian-born scientist who, as much as any single man, not excepting his friend, Albert Einstein, contributed to the development of nuclear energy. Indeed, with Enrico Fermi, he held the first patent on the atomic chain reaction. It was he who made known to Einstein the practical possibilities of an atomic explosion. When the Second World War ended, he began a crusade for control of nuclear weapons—and, in fact, for control of war itself—a crusade that was to dominate the rest of his life. He was an idea factory, turning out all sorts of intricate notions and schemes for keeping the arms race from putting an end to the human race. Through it all, he never lost his effervescent belief in the possibilities of progress. He was a master of the incongruous and kept his friends amused by his ability to anatomize the ridiculous. How many sides there were to this man I was never able to calculate. He was without question one of the dozen greatest scientists of the age, his work embracing nuclear physics, chemistry, microbiology, biology, and radiology. The probing quality of his mind knew few modern counterparts. One invention on which he worked for many years eluded him. He wanted to invent peace.

BERTRAND RUSSELL: spare, crusty, pipe-smoking. He climbed the heights of mathematical and philosophical abstractions as did few other intellectual figures of his time. He leaned heavily on the work of Alfred North Whitehead and Ludwig Wittgenstein, or at least that portion of their work that broke with traditional thought. He became deeply involved in political and moral issues and had even more influence outside England than in his own homeland. Personally, he could be playful and even impish. Those of his friends who expected him to be quixotic and inconsistent were seldom disappointed. In the company of other eminent intellects he could be uncommunicative at times to the point of inarticulateness. When he met Albert Schweitzer for the first time at the home of a mutual friend in London, what was expected to be an historic intellectual encounter turned out to be an epic non-event. Russell commented on the weather, which in London has seldom made for exciting conversation. Schweitzer nodded affably. Absolute silence and small talk alternated for the next few minutes, then Russell looked at his watch and said it was time to leave for the country. If Schweitzer felt deprived because the discussion did not turn on Russell's favorite themes—agnosticism, equality of the sexes, non-totalitarian socialism, and free love—he carefully concealed his loss. Russell's antipathy to orthodoxy and his talent for intricate grammar were perhaps never better demonstrated than in his *Our Knowledge of the External World,* when he wrote: "The one and only condition, I believe, which is necessary in order to secure for philosophy in the near future an achievement that surpasses all that has hitherto been accomplished by philosophers, is the creation of a school of men with scientific training and philosophical interests, unhampered by the traditions of the past, and not misled by the literary methods of those who copy the ancients in all except their merits."

THE PRIVILEGE OF KNOWING Grenville Clark was deeply felt. I knew no private citizen who exercised greater influence over the history of his times. He was a lawyer whose advice on matters far beyond the law was sought out by at least five presidents, by cabinet officers, Supreme Court justices and members of Congress. He made me think of Americans like Madison, Jefferson, and John Adams. His political philosophy was in the tradition of John Stuart Mill, the Physiocrats, leaders of the Philadelphia Constitutional Convention, and jurists like Oliver Wendell Holmes.

In 1945, Grenville Clark was one of the few men in the world who foresaw that the newly won peace would soon be threatened by an atomic arms race. He believed the moment in history had come for creating the instruments of a world authority, with limited but adequate powers for dealing with the causes of war and atomic weaponry. Together with Supreme Court Justice Owen Roberts he summoned a group of forty-eight Americans to his home in Dublin, New Hampshire, to draft a statement that was to serve as the effective beginning of the movement for world peace through world law. The "Dublin Declaration" became the basis for a major contribution to the literature on world peace. Grenville Clark collaborated with Louis B. Sohn in writing a book which has since become a standard in its field, *World Peace Through World Law.*

Listening to Grenville Clark in any conference was an

unforgettable experience. His very presence often changed the tenor of the discussions, as happened at the "Darmouth Conference" exchange between prominent citizens of the U.S. and U.S.S.R. He demonstrated not just the power of logic but the prodigious force represented by an understanding of the next person's experience and problems. He proved, moreover, that the most hardened positions tend to dissolve in the presence of honest good will and friendliness. Grenville Clark had a vision of a better world, and he did as much as any person, public or private, to try to make it real.

FOR A HALF DECADE OR MORE, the most powerful man in the United States was not the president but Henry A. Kissinger. What was the source of his wide influence and his direct access to history-in-the-making? He had never held elective office. He had no constituency. Yet he was able to accomplish deeds in the field of U.S. foreign policy that had eluded the efforts of seasoned statesmen. The key to Kissinger was that he had theories about history that emerged from his intensive studies of the complex and chaotic experiences of nineteenth-century Europe, culminating in the Congress of Vienna. His conclusion was that notions of clear-cut victory or unconditional surrender were illusory. In the end, there were always conditions. In his mind, the best settlement between contending parties was one in which neither side would be an absolute victor or absolute loser. This didn't make for an uncomplicated peace, but then again, he felt that history was never very tidy; the art of world politics was the avoidance of supposedly perfect solutions. Extrication was often to be preferred to supposedly glorious triumphs. This was the philosophy behind the withdrawal from Vietnam. The settlement he negotiated and for which he won the Nobel Peace Prize was not a settlement that added fresh laurels to a nation that had never lost a war. But it extricated the United States from a situation that it got into through miscalculation and that was tearing the country apart. The arrangements he made between Egypt and Israel didn't resolve the underlying questions; but they created a process that accepted negotiations, however inconclusive, as preferable to open conflict. His trip to the People's Republic of China cleared the way for the new relationship between the countries. Basically, his main genius was as an engineer of consent. He was able to persuade people that movement in the direction he wanted them to go was actually an advance towards their ultimate needs and goals.

In 1969, I was involved in a project to bring medical relief to the Biafran people in the Nigerian Civil War. We couldn't get the kind of cooperation we needed from the U.S. State Department to move food and medical supplies into the war zone. I went to Kissinger for help. He removed the road-blocks—and did it so adroitly that the supplies and transportation facilities put at our disposal became an implementation rather than a contradiction of U.S. foreign policy. I doubt if I have ever known anyone who better understood the principle that in world affairs the shortest distance between two points is often a labyrinth.

He was probably one of the three or four most complex and fascinating figures of the twentieth century. To someone such as myself, who grew up as an admirer of Woodrow Wilson ("open covenants openly arrived at") Henry Kissinger at first seemed to me to be far too Bismarckian for my taste. But I came to realize that he was a man of extraordinary talents who knew that the subtlest differentiations were vital ingredients in the making of essential progress. He never struck a pose of idealism but welcomed the company of idealists. They came to him for help; generally, he found a way to help them achieve their purposes—and he hoped they would be wise enough to proclaim no triumphs.

6

Ways of Seeing

IT WAS HORACE SUTTON, a colleague at the *Saturday Review,* who introduced me to cameras. The year was 1950 or 1951. He made it possible for me to stretch my vision and develop new ways of seeing things. As a child, I had discovered that I could change the shape of clouds and trees through squinting the imagination. Now I learned how to make the camera squint along with me. The camera's flexibility consisted of its varying combinations of light and shutter speed, and its ability to see deeply into things or to focus narrowly. I became aware that trees had faces and that their barks revealed an infinity of abstract designs, all of them leaping to life in the imagination. I became a collector of skyscapes. Riding high above the clouds, I became transfixed by spectacles that had been denied me below. There were vast mountains of ice and white silk; there were long caverns turning magenta when hit by sudden shafts of light that were like slivers off the sun.

This is not to say that these were the only attractions. I became fascinated with people on park benches. The park bench is a world of its own, a fellowship which joins all those who cherish surcease from frenzy and who are not too eager to get too soon to where they have to go. It is a good place to talk about things that may never happen. "The business of philosophy," Oliver Wendell Holmes wrote, "is to show that we are not fools for doing what we want to do."

Other favorites—lonely figures against the background of long stretches of beach or landscape; elderly people, especially in places of worship; diagonals that dominate any design of which they are a part; spunky seagulls chasing receding waves; overhead wires converging in the distance; families posing for pictures.

A man comes to know himself through the pictures he takes. Just in the process of reviewing the hundreds of pictures I have taken over the years in many parts of the world, I learn some things about the texture of my own responses—conscious and subconscious. The camera is more than a box that records an external situation; it is also turned inwards. The two sides to a film are not just negative and positive; they are the object photographed and the mind that reveals itself when confronted by this object.

This section seeks to record some visual notes for this "autobiography." It includes—appropriately, I think—photographs of two photographers for whom I have deep affection, Margaret Bourke-White and Yousef Karsh.

TWA's terminal at JFK Airport in New York was not merely built, it was sculpted. The ramplike passageway is an ethereal journey in itself.

Looking south from the Pan American building. New York City's Park Avenue South is like a carpet leading to a cluster of magic mountains.

Years after the Second World War, Berlin was still in ruins. Anyone who has seen the rubble of a city that has been destroyed by bombing knows that the human race is on notice, that nothing we do individually or collectively makes sense unless it is connected to the making of a structured peace.

Discord and disintegration have gone on for so long in Northern Ireland that by 1981 they have become a way of life. People find themselves adjusting to things that human beings should never be expected to adjust to.

Grenville Clark was one of the wisest—and greatest—men I ever met. He had instant access to and enormous influence with leading public figures in the United States for almost half a century. He possessed all the arts of genuine friendship, among which are how to listen and how to guide without pushing. I have always felt that his sense of history, his judiciousness, his analytic intelligence, and his ability to work with people would have made him a great president of the United States.

Bucky Fuller's public trademark is the geodesic dome. But his own preference would probably be a sailing mast. He is proud of his navy background in World War I. He spends part of each summer at his island in Penobscot Bay, Maine, and counts that day lost when he is not at the helm of his sailing ship. When I arrived, he rushed up to me, his eyes dancing behind his thick glasses. "Something incredibly wonderful has happened," he exulted. "I just discovered the coordinates to the universe." My congratulations were quite sincere.

Aboard U.S. Air Force One, in December 1966, Hubert H. Humphrey made no effort to conceal or even subdue his playfulness. We were on our way to the Far East to represent the president at the inauguration ceremonies of Ferdinand Marcos as president of the Philippines and to go on from there for the purpose of exploring the possibilities of a negotiated peace in the Vietnam War.

At his farm in Gettysburg, just a few months after completing his term in the presidency, Dwight D. Eisenhower talked about his favorite hobby—painting. "When I paint, I have the feeling that my eyes are reborn. I now see things that I never saw before." Only toward the end of his presidency did he feel comfortable about leading the nation.

Yousuf Karsh. Elegant in manner and dress, he was infinitely curious about everything. I know I had my nerve asking one of the world's great portrait photographers if I could take his picture. He agreed, so long as he didn't have to pose. This photograph was taken in 1961.

Margaret Bourke-White. This photograph was taken just a few months before she learned that the reason she kept falling was that she had Parkinson's disease. But her hands remained steady for many months, and she continued at her profession. Inevitably, there came the day when strapping the camera to her arm no longer enabled her to take unblurred photographs. She was one of the most courageous human beings I've ever known—and one of the loveliest.

Pope John in St. Peter's, at his last canonization ceremony (1963). "I know I am just a man. But not everyone else knows, so I have to remind them." Later, he said: "Nuclear war is not just a war between nations; it is a war of man against God."

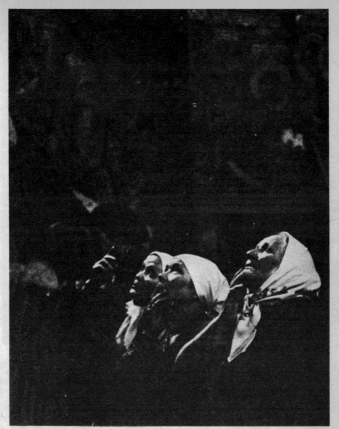

Kiev Cathedral. I was outside the cathedral when my wife rushed up to me to tell me about the three women inside the church who seemed transported by their experience of it. I reloaded my camera on the run. Inside, it was dark—too dark, I feared, even for fast film. Then, suddenly, the women crossed a shaft of filtered light and stopped transfixed, as they gazed upward. Not until the film was returned by the developers did I know whether the light was adequate (even though I stepped down the speed of the lens to 1/15 second). Edward Steichen did me the high honor of asking for a print for his own collection.

The colonnade at St. Peter's. The cobblestones and the columns provide a classical backdrop for this promenade by two friars.

Romania. About fifty miles from Bucharest we came across a convent where the nuns prepared one of the most delicious meals we have ever experienced. Across the garden was a nun framed against a convent wall, the apertures of which were like notes in a Beethoven symphony.

Premier Nikita Kruschchev at his retreat in Gagra, on the Black Sea, April 1963. He was especially proud of his glass-enclosed swimming pool with its retractable roof. When I remarked that I knew of no pool with such advanced features in the United States, he replied, straight-faced: "Cheer up, you belong to a young and ingenious society. Your country will have one in due course." At Gagra, I tried, on behalf of President Kennedy, to clear away some of the misunderstandings about the American position on the proposed Nuclear Test Ban Treaty.

Leningrad. A park bench is still the world's favorite community center.

New memories are being created.

Memories are the privilege of the old.

Hiroshima reborn. Not more than a couple of miles from the center of the nuclear explosion of August 6, 1945, a new industry burgeons. The Mazda rotary-engine automobile plant made Hiroshima a major industrial center.

ATOMIC BOMB CENTER
OUTLINE OF DAMAGE

ON 9 AUGUST 1945, AT 11.02 A.M. AN ATOMIC BOMB EXPLODED IN THE AIR JUST ABOVE HERE. INSTANTEOUSLY, ALL THE HOUSES IN THIS URAKAMI AREA COLLAPSED. THERE WAS A TREMENDOUS CONFLAGRATION.

OTHER PARTS OF NAGASAKI CITY WERE ALSO BURNT DOWN AND PRACTICALLY ALL THE HOUSES IN THE CITY SUFFERED HALF DESTRUCTION BY THE EXPLOSIVE WIND.

THE PITIABLE SCENE WAS BEYOND DESCRIPTION. THE OUTLINE BY MEANS OF FIGURE IS GIVEN HERE.
1. BURNT AREA   73.116000 SQ FT
2. DAMAGED HOUSES
   (TOTAL & MAJOR DESTRUCTION ONLY) 18.409 HOUSES
   TOTALLY BURNT 11.574 TOTALLY COLLAPSED 1326
   MAJOR DESTRUCTION 5509
3. SUFFERERS : 120.820 PERSONS
   DEATH 73.884 INJURED (INCLUDING LATER DEATHS
   CAUSED BY ATOMIC DISEASE) 76.796

On permanent exhibition in Nagasaki, site of the second atomic bombing, are this clock, which stopped at the instant of the explosion and has told no other time since, and a poster prepared by the city officials detailing the results of the bombing.

Evidence of the power of the Hiroshima explosion was easy to find in the early years after the atomic bombing. This piece of metal had melted in the heat released by the nuclear fission and then hardened again.

In 1953, a group of young women known as the "Hiroshima Maidens" were brought to the United States for reconstructive surgery. Fifteen years later, they came together in Hiroshima for reunion with some of their visiting American friends. Among the Japanese males in the photograph are Mayor Watanabe, the Reverend Kiyoshi Tanimoto, counselor to the young ladies, and Dr. Harada and Dr. Ouchi, Japanese physicians who were prominently associated with the Maidens project.

Street scene in Hiroshima in the early years after World War II. Nothing about the rehabilitation of Hiroshima was more symbolic to me than the disposition of the people and their ability to get on with the business of living.

上下水道　衛生設備　井戸ポンプ
小金井市指定水道工事店
中屋工業所
TEL(0423)⑧0873.2536

The clothes washline makes the entire world kin. I took this photograph in Hong Kong, Taiwan, or Japan.

Peking. The national palaces and museums take on the appearance at times of children's playgrounds. Few things seem more characteristic of the nation than the omnipresence of youngsters.

The strong father-son tradition in Japan takes a Western accent. In Kyoto, where the cultural and religious heritage is visibly apparent, this father seemed pleased to pose for a photograph.

One of the most memorable scenes of my 1968 visit to the Albert Schweitzer Hospital in Africa. This tableau, with Dr. Schweitzer at the right, was occasioned by the departure of a nurse for a sabbatical in Europe.

Even at 90, Albert Schweitzer was fully functional physically and intellectually. The only thing that made him feel old, he said, was his inability to answer his mail. He would receive hundreds of letters each week; he did his best to answer all of them but kept falling behind. It got to a point where anyone who didn't write to him was his friend.

Dr. Margaret van der Kreek, a young physician from Holland, at the Schweitzer Hospital. "Here at Lamabarene," she said, "we do very nicely without the frills, and we never have to ask ourselves, 'Are we really needed?'"

"We have no intention," said Dr. Schweitzer, "of running a hospital that looks as if it had been designed in America or Europe. What we have done here is to build an African village and connect to it a clinic. The people who come here are not terrified by strange sights. They feel at home. While they are here, we make their relatives a part of the hospital staff."

During the Biafran War (1969), the principal problem was not just providing food for homeless children but finding a place of safety for them. The scars in the concrete wall came from mortar fire. After everything was done for the children that could be done, there were still the unanswered questions in their eyes for us to think about.

One of the most spectacularly beautiful drives in the world is in the vicinity of the Baggio in the Philippines. Not far from the terraced rice fields one comes upon this specimen of Gothic-like architecture.

News of the Americans landing on the moon was the vehicle of the imagination that enabled people throughout the world to share in the experience. This picture was taken in Doula (Cameroons) about two weeks after the moon landing of the Apollo Space Flight.

All Johannesburg seemed to be caught up in a balancing act, symbolized by this young lady.

This gentleman lived on a farm near Lahore, Pakistan. He was the only one in a family of seven who survived the communal rioting that accompanied the partition of India. No one knows how many millions of people lost their lives in that period of upheaval. Lifelong friends suddenly found themselves in hand-to-hand combat. It would take another Tolstoi to master all the dramatic materials that were bound up in that conflict.

In America it is jogging; in China, Tai Chi. Not far from our hotel in Canton was a public park where, each morning, shortly after sunup, hundreds of people practice the art of slow motion rhythm exercise. One of the arguments for Tai Chi is that it helps to take the sharp edges out of life and does not ignore the mind in ministering to the muscle.

Education is one of the principal preoccupations of the Filipino people. Schools abound everywhere: in the cities, dental and medical colleges and law schools advertise vigorously for students, while in the rural areas, adult education classes never wait for eager customers.

Nude about to ascend the stairs. The place is Laos, the time is 1961, and a war is just around the corner. The Hormel can cover is through the courtesy of the U.S. Army.

7

The Cosmic Classroom

THE PROCESS OF GROWING UP as a species is not too different from the process of growing up as an individual. We come of age as a cosmic species when we accept the fact that the universe does not exist for our exclusive convenience. The first big jolt to the species' ego came when Copernicus discovered that the earth is not the center of all things. Even after the human species adjusted to the Copernican reality, it persisted in believing that the universe was designed with human life at the center. Now we must make our peace with the reality that, though we may be a highly privileged species, we may not be one of a kind. We must adjust, finally, to the fact that the universe may not be constructed for our particular benefit.

Far from feeling diminished, we should feel a sense of privilege. A great adventure opens out before us. We have new worlds to contemplate. We have new connections to make. A rendezous with infinity becomes us.

IN A RELATIVE SENSE, life is still rare enough to suit the most demanding species' ego. But what is important is that, whatever its place in infinity, life is infinitely precious. It is precious because of what it is, not because of any universal prevalence it may have.

It is precious because the human mind can contemplate questions such as these. We do not have to experience infinity in order to encompass it.

It is precious because we have access to the phenomenon of cause and effect, thus being able to create our own causes and to shape our own effects. We can dwell on the experiences of past lives and thus enhance our own time.

It is precious not because it is perfectible but because human beings can comprehend the idea of perfectibility. It is precious because there are no limits to the fineness of human sensitivities. We are capable of responding to the good, the true, and the beautiful. We have the capacity to love and to respond to love.

It is precious because we can continue to create in ways we have never created before. We can do the impossible.

Finally, nothing about human life is more precious than that we can define our own destiny.

It is only a few hundred years since the human species was able to liberate itself from the notion that the earth was the center of the universe. The larger perspective afforded by Copernicus played an important part in the forward thrust of human development. The Age of Reason and the Age of the Enlightenment were not unrelated to that discovery. But we are only now beginning to possess a genuine awareness of our relationship to the total scheme of things; and we can expect that human progress will be proportionate to our comprehension of our place in the universal design.

OUR SPACESHIPS ARE IMPORTANT not because they are capable of breaking out of the earth's gravitational field but because they are extensions of the human mind. They are not so much an assemblage of lightweight metals as they are a new language. This language speaks to human potentiality and to new options available to us as a nation and as a species. Every new experience, every new adventure, yields a new harvest in language. The words produced by our forays into the universe will transcend technology.

TO PARAPHRASE H. G. WELLS, human history has been a race between combat and cooperation, between concepts of power and concepts of service. If the outcome of that race is not to end in disaster, new unifying principles have to be put into effect. The species must develop a sense of the whole, a reverence for its life-support systems, and an understanding of the limitless capacity of human beings to meet any dangers within their comprehension. Knowledge is a solvent for danger.

"TWO THINGS FILL THE MIND with ever-new and increasing wonder and awe," wrote Immanuel Kant, "the starry heavens above and the moral law within me."

NOTHING IN THE UNIVERSE has more grandeur than the infinity of the human mind. Even pea-size computers capable of forecasting the movement of the galaxies are not more wondrous than the mysterious human creature that produced them. The ultimate frontier is not geographical or spatial but intellectual.

THE SAME CONDITIONS that make life possible make life inevitable. Yet our collective ego blurs our view and we don't ask the primary question. The primary question should be: How did the conditions that make life possible originate? How did they come altogether in vital confluence? The interaction of these precise and exquisite conditions forces life into being. So long as these conditions continue to interact, life is inevitable. Infinity supplies the stage.

OUR OWN DEFICIENCIES—or limitations in our own faculties of observation or methods of observation—affect our idea of the universe. Our tiny universe may be lost in infinity, but it operates and has an essence. And even within the universe itself, the separate parts or aspects may seem so minute as to be nonexistent within the whole, but each of these parts has its own significance. Each of these parts is none the less functional for being swallowed up in infinity.

THE SOLAR SYSTEM is not unique. Nature shuns one of a kind. It is unreasonable and unscientific to say that throughout the numberless celestial systems there are no other planets which support life in advanced form. If this idea is difficult to accept, all we have to do is to enlarge our idea of infinity by as many billions of planets as may be required to accommodate the belief that highly differentiated life forms exist—or even abound—in the universe. Infinity applies both to space and time. If anything occurs at one place or at one time in the universe, it is bound to occur in another, given infinite time and infinite space. The possible becomes the inevitable whenever there are no limits on laws of chance.

EVEN IF OUR UNIVERSE is nothing more than a tiny speck in infinity, it is large enough to have vital significance through the interaction of life and, in a larger sense, the interaction of all time, space, matter, and energy. We may never be able to prove in absolute terms that life is not an illusion but it is within our capacity to comprehend that there is a consequential reality and that this reality depends less on dimension than on interrelationship and effect.

THE MORE THE HUMAN SPECIES pushes back the frontiers of space and the more its capacity for awe is stretched as a result, the more certain it is that the most mysterious and wondrous object in the entire universe is human life itself. Our scientific research serves mainly to enlarge our respect for what remains to be learned about life.

PERSPECTIVE CAN HELP US not just to ponder ironies but to cope with them. It is a spectacular feat of intelligence to listen to a man's heartbeat on the moon and to be able to calibrate the precise amount of straining his heart is under; but what about the hearts of men on earth? Are we fully tuned into the human heart where we are? How much unnecessary heartbreak is caused because the earth has yet to be made into a fit habitat for most of its humans?

"THERE IS NO EASY ROAD," Seneca wrote, "from the earth to the stars." No road, that is, except the human mind.

ANYTHING THAT IGNITES the human mind, anything that sets the collective intelligence to racing, anything that creates a new horizon for human hopes, anything that helps to enlarge the vocabulary of common heritage and common destiny—anything that does this is of incalculable value.

Some people will say we have no business in journeying beyond the planet until we make our own abode on earth safe and fit for human habitation. Yet it is precisely because our species is in jeopardy that we have to think and act on a universal plane rather than as members of hostile tribes. A rendezvous with the cosmos is a transcendent occasion and could become a transcendent process.

FOR ALL OUR LOFTY philosophical excursions, we are still earthbound. We are overly fond of applying concepts about size, direction, time, space, and energy to situations in which those concepts may be completely extraneous. We are measurement-minded. Our plane of existence necessarily utilizes such concepts. Yet there is a larger plane on which those approaches may have no validity.

ONLY HUMAN BEINGS have the capacity to define goals and to attempt to meet them. Only they possess the quality to inspire and be inspired. Only they know the meaning and the power of conscience. Only they can contemplate their own nature and the nature of the universe and conceive of a higher nature than either. But with all our faculties, we have been unable as a species to cope with ourselves. In the midst of the potential splendor of orderly existence we are paupers chained to chaos.

HUMAN LIFE IS THE RAREST, most complex, and most precious of all the prizes in the universe. It is this prize that is now in the process of being diminished and rejected—by humans themselves. Humans are tampering with the vital fractions that make their existence possible. It becomes necessary, therefore, to develop a survival perspective. We must think in ways we have never thought before—about our uniqueness, about our place in the universe, about the preciousness of life, about value, about our relationship to other human beings, about the new institutions or mechanisms that are required to deal with random and pulverizing power, and about the rights of the next generation.

IN OUR TIME, the liberation of human beings from earth gravity has enabled the species to become less theoretical about, and detached from, the universe. What was most significant about the lunar voyage was not that men set foot on the moon but

that they set eye on the earth. They perceived larger relationships. They had an increased sense of human uniqueness. The
effect was philosophical. To be able to rise from the earth; to
be able, from a station in outer space, to see the relationship of
the planet earth to other planets; to be able to contemplate the
billions of factors which in a precise and beautiful combination
make human existence possible; to be able to meditate on journeying through an infinity of galaxies; to be able to dwell upon
an encounter of the human brain and spirit with the universe—
all this creates a new human horizon. It also offers proof that
technology is subordinate to human imagination. We went to
the moon not because of our technology but because of our
imagination.

IT IS UNSCIENTIFIC and unrealistic to believe that men who have
solved the problem of leaping across space to inspect the face
of Mars lack the wit to create vital balances on earth.

WE HAVE TRIED to throw our arms around infinity and have
been left not with the universe in our arms but with a closed
and empty circle. Hence the more we know, the more confused
we become. Boundlessness and endlessness at first fascinate
then appall us.

THE "SOMETHING" that constitutes human uniqueness cannot
adequately be described by any single term. Even "man's spirit"
and "capacity for faith"—however poetic and evocative—are
not the sum total of that uniqueness. Perception, awareness,
and conscience represent other elements of human uniqueness
without exhausting them. Love, compassion, and sense of
brotherhood are characteristics within human capacity, but
they, too, are part of a larger whole. Similarly, intelligence,
imagination, command of historical experience, and ability to
inspire and be inspired are other parts of this whole but are not
the whole itself.

　　Just as it is necessary to think of infinity as lacking a specific
form or even a specific substance, so human uniqueness defies
mere verbalization and exists in its combined manifestations.

One might also say that this uniqueness is manifest in existence itself.

IF IT IS ASKED what we get in return for our probes in space, the answer is that we get a chance to develop a proper appreciation for our station in the universe. It is also quite possible that such ventures might bring the world's peoples a little closer to one another. Americans can congratulate themselves that they are in a position to take giant steps beyond their planet—not just for themselves but for the astonishingly varied, gifted, frail, and vulnerable species of which they are a part.

THE SCRAPINGS FROM the surface of the moon brought back to earth, significant as they are, are not as meaningful as the perceptions carried back in our minds. The biggest moon divided is an enlarged awareness of the rarity of human life. We also possess new evidence of our ability to adjust to ever-increasing complexity. In this sense, what outer space has most to offer humans is an increased respect for the importance of inner space and for the workings of the mind.

The human brain is a mirror to infinity. There is no limit to its range, scope, or creative growth. New perspectives lead to new perceptions, just as they clear the way for all sorts of new prospects in human affairs. No one knows what great leaps of achievement may be within the reach of the species once the full potentiality of the mind is developed. As we create an ever-higher sense of our cosmic consciousness, we become aware of our ever-higher possibilities and challenges.

THE YEN TO BECOME WANDERERS among the stars involves more than the need to satisfy a cosmic curiosity. Basically, it flows out of an instinctive need to evolve. We belong to an unfinished species. We have limitless capacities for growth; indeed, our uniqueness lies in our ability to steer our own evolution. The destination becomes visible through an enlarged perspective. The greatest adventure within the reach of a sentient species is seeing itself in an expanding relationship. The creatures in Plato's allegory of the cave could not conceive of anything beyond their constricted domain and therefore were consigned to and limited by a perpetual darkness. We have no way of knowing how much new light we can let into our lives or the corners of our minds by breaking out of our cave, but there can be no doubt that we will be changed in the process.

THE EARTH DWELLERS, whether they live in eastern or western hemispheres, have not prepared themselves adequately for the journey into space. We have directed our attention to machinery rather than motives. We have been concerned with blast-off when we should have been thinking about basic purpose. In a more general sense, our education bears all of the marks of specific earth gravity. We have been part of the cosmos but we have tended to regard it as scenery rather than a total abode. Copernicus, Einstein, and Shapley notwithstanding, man still sees man as the center of the universe. We have cheapened our goals by cutting them down to accessible size and separating them from a concept beyond infinity. It is as though we had been preparing for Beethoven by listening to hyenas.

THE JOURNEY INTO SPACE IS, or should be, a sublime experience. The selection of astronauts ought not to be confined to men in the military or in technology. Why not poets, philosophers, or theologians? If it is said that space has stern physical requirements, the problem can be met. There are strapping fellows among those who have demonstrated their capacity to think creatively and who have some convictions about the nature of man. One of the prime requisites for an astronaut is not just his ability to follow a specified procedure and to take measurements but to be able to be at one with a new environment. A space ship requires true perspective. This is nothing that can be imparted in a course on astronautics; it comes with the responsible development of intellect and insight. A respect for the human spirit may be even more important than a knowledge of centrifugal force. Moreover, a certain artistry is called for when man proposes to range the universe. It is an artistry both of personal response and ability to communicate. For when the astronaut returns to earth his message should be more than an excited series of remarks on a fabulous journey.

The returning messenger should have the ability to impart a sense of great new connections that may transform life as we have known it.

WHETHER OR NOT interplanetary communications ever materialize, an even more grandiose project awaits us. This is the need for human beings to communicate with one another, here and now.

The lack of respect for a common human destiny continues to be the main problem of the earth dwellers. To the extent that they fix their gaze and energies on this need they will qualify themselves for survival.

THE IDEA OF MAN IN SPACE is an explosion of the imagination. It shakes loose the sense of wonder; it cracks open a vast area of the human potential; it confronts the intelligence with the infinite. But it also adds to the terror. Not terror of what is unknown about space but of what is known about man. A great ascent has taken place without any corresponding elevation of ideas. We have raised our station without raising our sights. We roam the heavens with the engines of hell.

PHILOSOSOPHY IS NEVER a finished garment. One grows into it. Year by year individuals are shaped by the sights, the sounds, the ideas around them. Consciously or not, we are forever adding to or substracting from the sum total of our beliefs, attitudes, or responses, or whatever it is we mean when we say that a person has a certain outlook on life. It is one of the prime glories of the human mind that the same idea or experience is never absorbed in precisely the same way by any two individuals who may be exposed to it.

Each human being is a process—a filtering process of retention or rejection, absorption or loss. The process gives a person individuality. It determines whether one lies and dies without having been affected by the beauty of wonder and the wonder of beauty, without having had any real awareness of kinship or human fulfillment.

PHILOSOPHY SEEKS TO MAKE connections in the human mind between the memories of the race and the ways of thinking about life. It constructs principles for asking meaningful questions and for disciplining the speculations those question produce. But the test of philosophy is its ability to contribute to its own time while remaining independent of it.

IMAGINATION INCLUDES OUR ABILITY as human beings to raise prodigiously the threshold of our awareness so that we see ourselves for what we really are—individuals in the immortal body of humankind. This gift of imagination, combined with knowledge, enables us to do more than participate only theoretically in the lives of those who have lived before us. Through the art of creative reading, for example, the panorama of history is spread before us. The grand individual experiences in history can be reborn and fulfilled in the imagination.

The past is dead only for those who lack the desire to bring it to life.

GOD STANDS IN FULLEST GLORY not when made to sit astride infinity or when regarded as an architect of cosmic spectacles, but when contemplated as the ultimate force that prevents the cosmic void from being complete.

Whether the Great Design of Creation exists within a microcosm or macrocosm is unimportant; the vital particles inside it have order and purpose and exist. And there is a place inside that order for humanity, for consciousness, for conscience, for love. This is what is important. We are not children of relativity. We are children of God. And we are brothers. We enjoy or suffer the consequences of our ideas, our acts, our hopes, and our fears.

IMMORTALITY IS NOT a distant and shiny phenomenon but a living reality. You live in others; others live in you. So long as any human being lives you have life. Your passport to immortality, to be valid, must have the stamp of the human community upon it.

WE CAN TALK ABOUT CREATION, we can talk about the nature of life, even about the nature of nature. But all this only sets the stage for the ultimate answer man seeks—which is about him self. Man may be fascinated with ultimate causes but he is more than fascinated—he is concerned—about ultimate destination; in particular, personal destination. The quest of immortality may be an even stronger common element among the great religions of the world than the Golden Rule.

THE LONGING FOR IMMORTALITY is as nearly universal as anything we know pertaining to the inner wishes of human beings. Some men, from time to time, have renounced any interest in the subject of immortality. They are lost, however, in the vastness of the general quest.

WE ARE WIDE-EYED when contemplating the possibility that life may exist elsewhere in the universe, but we wear blinders when contemplating the possibilities of life on earth.

PERSPECTIVE CONTINUES TO BE our greatest shortage, just as our ironies continue to be our most abundant product.

CRAMPED NOTIONS OF INFINITY tend to construct speculations about the cosmos, and we fail to ask the primary question. The primary question is not, "Where did life come from?" but "What can human life become?"

TRUE NOTHINGNESS IS IMPOSSIBLE. Infinity would swallow us up but it cannot. Nothingness surrounds us but it cannot claim us. The rejection of nothingness is the most significant fact about the cosmos, just as it is the most significant fact about life. Not even science can conceive of pure nothingness; pure nothingness exists nowhere. The universe may be only a particle but it asserts itself and nothingness is kept from becoming absolute. Thus the universe is a vital particle. And there are vital particles inside it, the most vital of which is human beings.

SCIENCE DISCOVERS THE BIG QUESTIONS; philosophy relates them. Science does the sorting; philosophy the connecting.

WE MAY HAVE NO JURISDICTION over the fact of our existence, but we hold supreme command over the meaning of that existence.

OUR ETERNAL QUEST AS HUMAN BEINGS is to shatter our loneliness. It is this quest that enables philosophers and theologians to make common cause with poets and artists. Loneliness is multidimensional. There is the loneliness of mortality. There is the loneliness of time that passes too slowly or too swiftly. There is the loneliness of inevitable separation. There is the loneliness of alienation. There is the loneliness of aspiration. There is the loneliness of squandered dreams. There is the collective loneliness of the species, unable to proclaim its oneness in a world chained to its tribalisms.

And now, finally, there is the loneliness of life in the universe, always a philosophical preoccupation but now a presiding reality reinforced by man's forays into space. The change is greater than was represented by the Copernican revolution. Copernicus's contribution was primarily to knowledge, only secondarily to philosophy. After Copernicus, there was the challenge to the human mind that came from knowing that the earth was not the center of all things—but this challenge did not substantially change the fact that man continued to see himself as the hub of the universe. People were astounded that previous generations should ever have believed that the earth did not revolve around the sun—but they continued to live in an anthropocentric world in an abstract universe.

THE QUESTION OF REALITY versus illusion cannot be decided by objective proof because the examining mechanism is the mind of man and man is part of that which he seeks to examine. Objective proof in this case would have to come from something outside the ken or scope of man. Man may enlarge his objective techniques and even his knowledge, but he cannot change the basic fact that his position in contemplating the great questions is inherently subjective.

LIFE IS RICH in its consequences. Consequences give reality to man's capacity to struggle between good and evil, nobility and venality, altruism and selfishness. We fashion our consequences as surely as we fashion our goods or our dwellings. Nothing we say, think, or do is without its consequences. Just as there is no loss of basic energy in the universe, so no thought or action is without its effects, present or ultimate, seen or unseen, felt or unfelt. Reality *is* consequences. At every stop in life we are coping with the consequences of ideas and actions, most of them long since forgotten. These consequences or effects are the unseen factors in individual life and the affairs of man; they are imponderables only in the sense that they are not directly identified. But they are no less vital than that which is explicit and accessible in human experience. In short, life is of consequence—literally so. Wisdom consists of the anticipation of consequences.

THE SIGNIFICANCE OF LIFE is not to be found in theories of illusion or reality but in life itself. Our lack of an objective position from which we can contemplate ourselves need not cripple us philosophically or spiritually. Whatever the nature of the universe of which we are a part, we have a mind and a body that interact with other minds and bodies. That interaction has consequences, good and bad. And it is to the fact of such consequences that we most profitably can address ourselves. What is truly meaningless is preoccupation with the "meaninglessness of existence." We may not be able to prove objectively what we are or what we are part of, but such objective proof is of minor importance alongside the fact of interaction and consequence.

IN T. S. ELIOT'S *The Cocktail Party*, the leading character asks, "What is hell?" Then he proceeds to supply his own answer: "Hell is oneself. Hell is alone, the other figures in it merely projections. There is nothing to escape from and nothing to escape to. One is always alone." Later another character in Mr. Eliot's play supplements this concept of hell by picturing it as "the final desolution of solitude in the phantasmal world of imagination, shuffling memories, and desires."

THERE IS ANOTHER HELL beyond the hell in which "one is always alone," in Eliot's phrase. It is a hell in which we succeed in piercing our loneliness, in establishing our bonds with others—only to discover a collective loneliness in the universe. The iron walls of the self may be torn down in a magnificent triumph of common purpose and common conscience as we discover we are but single cells in a larger and common body. But it is not enough. For hell begins where larger identification stops. No loneliness is as great as that which severs the society of human beings from identification with the totality of all life and all things.

"HELL BEGINS," Gian-Carlo Menotti has said, "on the day when God grants us a clear vision of all that we might have achieved, of all the gifts which we have wasted, of all that we might have done which we did not do. . . . For me, the conception of hell lies in two words: 'too late.' " How large is hell? Thoreau's answer: "No larger than a spark."

IT IS NOT TRUE that genius will always out. Genius can decay and destroy itself in the rust of its own corrosive juices. The retrospective hell over the unachieved is a small oven compared to the living hell of coping with a mysterious inner vault that volition alone cannot unlock.

SO LONG AS HUMANS are troubled by the excuses they make for themselves, there will be no dearth of definitions of hell. But one definition of hell that has persisted over the years is of a place where people have lost the capacity to recognize or respond to beauty.

WE NOW COME TO HELL'S OWN HELL. The torment experienced by those at this innermost station may not be easily described but at least the sufferers may be recognized. This is the hell of those who possess a natural idealism yet turn their backs on it; who know the meaning of nobility yet resist it; who can comprehend dignity yet shun it. Finally, it is the hell of those who have an awareness of what is meant by the gift of life yet fail to justify it.

8

Creative Options

THE WRITER IS A CREATOR OF OPTIONS. The writer enables people to discover new truths and new possibilities within themselves and to fashion new connections to human experience. Nothing is more vital for the creative artist than access to an audience. Repressive and insecure societies keep the artist under control not by forbidding him to write or paint but by separating him from his audience. What Solzhenitsyn protested was not that he was forbidden to write but that his writing was not available to his countrymen. And great audiences, as Walt Whitman reminded us, are necessary if we want to have great poets. It is the audience that ultimately has to uphold the values of the ivory tower.

THE ARTIST PROPERLY INSISTS on his right to express himself and to experiment as fully as he wishes. He does not believe he should be asked to explain what he means or to justify his belief that what he has produced deserves to be exhibited. But the art-loving public, even more than the artist or critic, holds the ultimate power.

NO ONE HAS EVER BEEN ABLE to define or synthesize that precarious, splendid, and perhaps untidy instant when a creative process begins. This is what the uniqueness of the artist is all about. Also, this is what the basic right of the artist is all about—the right to create even though he may not always know what he is doing. "It is meaningless to ask," John Dewey wrote, "what an artist, 'really' means by his product; he himself would find different meanings in it at different days and hours and in different stages of his own development."

THE SOCIETY THAT IS TROUBLED because the artist may not seem to know what he is doing is troubled about the wrong things.

The worry should be directed rather to the narrow and tangible deeds of men who claim always to know what they are about, who are suspicious of abstract thought, and who neither comprehend nor respond to the mysteries of the creative process that separate the men from the drones. There is such a thing, Alfred North Whitehead reminds us, as the "fallacy of misplaced concreteness." Progress in human society, as in the individual, has something to do with the early and perhaps the undeflected perception of new energies and prospects. These are the vital ingredients for a fine hour in human affairs and for a civilizing experience.

ARGUMENTS OVER THE IVORY TOWER versus the arena are usually a waste of time. They tend to juxtapose Art against Involvement. They assume that creativity never needs its champions, that there is no connection between the shape of the society and the condition of the arts, and that the world of ideas is somehow separate from the world in which great books are written or great music composed or canvases painted or great drama staged.

CREATIVITY CAN BE STIFLED or throttled not just by political juggernauts but also by brutality or wickedness or squalor. It is folly, therefore, to assume that the editor or the writer or the artist has no obligation to the conditions that make creativity possible.

THE CONDITIONS OF LIFE are inseparable from the conditions of art. The truly creative writer or artist never has to choose between the ivory tower and the arena. He moves freely from one to the other according to his needs and his concerns.

THE RELENTLESS EROSION of a great literary talent is more than a personal tragedy, more than a national sorrow. It is loss without end for humanity itself. Writers and poets make possible the mingling of minds beyond time and circumstance, opening themselves and humanity to a view of the eternal.

NO ONE NEED BE INTIMIDATED into a feeling of total nullity or grim acquiescence if he disagrees with critics in literature, art, music, or anything else. The individual has the best credentials in the world for reacting: He has his own taste buds. They may not coincide with those of others, but at least they are his own, and the more he uses them the keener they become. No critic of stature—whether in literature or art or music—expects other people to take leave of their individual senses. The critic applies his special training and knowledge to the work before him. He defines his standards. He sees himself as part of the total process by which a culture advances toward excellence. He certainly doesn't resent disagreement. And he doesn't discourage or disparage individual reactions—not if he is worth listening to, that is.

WHAT IS THE MOMENT of triumph for the author? It is the moment of conception. This is when an important idea is born, when there is a sudden glorious clicking of the vitals of the writer, when the creative wells are full and demanding release. It is also a moment of commitment, for the writer knows that the idea will possess him and hover over him until he puts down the words that will set him free again. If it is self-tyranny, it is at least the tyranny of purpose.

THE CREATIVE PROCESS depends least of all upon accident. It requires that the mind be properly worked and tended, that it be given the blessing of silence and the gift of sequence. Whether the moment of triumph produces a spark or a thunderbolt, it is certain to have lasting effects. It can generate the carrying power to sustain an author through a thousand nights of torment at the writing desk.

THE TROUBLE WITH SOME contemporary novels is that they are full of people not worth knowing. The characters slide in and out of the mind with hardly a ripple. They levy no tax on the memory; they make little claim on the connecting power of identification. They are always out in front of you, seldom inside you. When they suffer, you find yourself uncommitted and unengaged. They experiment with life rather than live it.

TOO MANY CURRENT NOVELS put situations ahead of people. It is felt, apparently, that characters exist for the purpose of accommodating a plot, thus minimizing the human potential and demonstrating the limitless possibilities of personal shrinkage. This is not the way to write good novels, much less great ones. There is nothing wrong with the audience; it is not true that people find the real world so dramatic that they can see no excitement in the product of a writer's imagination. Give readers a book with people they care about and they will queue up to shake the author's hand.

THE FAILURE OF SOME NOVELISTS to create real people can often be related to their failure to deal with the inner man. One suspects that some authors would rather be found dead than caught in the act of shedding an honest tear. Our main complaint is directed at the apparently increasing tendency of authors to stay outside rather than to explore the insides of their characters.

WE HAVE BEEN PASSING THROUGH what later historians will regard as the "Dry-Eyed Period of American Literature." The fear of sentimentalism has led to a retreat from honest sentimentality.

ONE OF THE GRAVE MALADIES of our time is the way sophistication seems to be valued above common sense. Words cease to have the plain meaning assigned to them and become wildly elastic. The manipulation of the idea seems to be more important than its integrity.

WHERE DO IDEALS COME FROM? How do they become tangible and far-reaching? The protector, the purveyor—indeed the germinator and generator—of ideals is the writer. This is his natural business. It is as difficult to separate ideals from the writer as it is to separate history from the historians. Milton, Paine, Garibaldi, Hugo, Montesquieu, Jefferson, Hume, Alfieri, Tennyson, Spinoza, Tagore, Iqbal, Confucius, Kagawa, John Stuart Mill—these are only a few writers who caused ideas and ideals to come full size in the reshaping of history.

WHAT IS IT we expect of the writer? We can certainly expect him to reflect the new spirit of the age, the spirit which points to human convergence. We can expect him to narrow the gap between the individual and society. We can expect him to shorten the distance between individual capacity and collective needs.

EFFECTIVE COMMUNICATIONS, oral or written, depend absolutely on a clear understanding of one's purpose. That purpose should be clearly identified. It should not be cluttered with extensive comment or side excursions. It should be developed point by point, with the rigorous attention to sequence and gradations of a professional bead-stringer at work.

THERE IS NEED FOR WRITERS who can restore to writing its powerful tradition of leadership in crisis. Most of the great tests in human history have produced great writers who acknowledged a special responsibility to their times. They defined the issues, recognized the values at stake, and dramatized the nature of the challenge. The central issue facing the world today is not the state of this nation or that nation but the condition of man. That higher level today needs its champions as it never did before. There is no more essential and nobler task for writers— established writers, new writers, aspiring writers—than to regard themselves as spokesmen for human destiny.

LANGUAGE IS NOT JUST an instrument but an environment. It is a vital part of the philosophical and political conditioning of a society. Attitudes are tied to the power of words to ennoble or condemn, augment or detract, glorify or demean. Negative language infects the human subconscious from the time a person first learns to speak. Prejudice is metabolized in the bloodstream of society.

ARISTOPHANES ONCE PROTESTED against what he called "traitors to the stage." He was referring to those writers who failed to make the most of the opportunities not just to entertain people but to change them and move them. The problem of the writer has always been to increase his usefulness and his accessibility. Brilliance of expression is not enough. The writer must have something to say. He must be able to get through. There can by no civilization without progress, no progress without ideas, no ideas without books. The writer helps to furnish the basic energy for human advance.

AT LEAST TWO EXPERIENCES are shared by every serious writer. The first is the yearning or determination to write his heart out in one Big Book, one that would fulfill itself and himself. The second is the dread of finality as represented not only by the difficulty in knowing when a book is finished but also the reluctance to part with it. A novel is a possessing embryo which consumes the imagination and drains the mind. But it also nourishes and replenishes. Thus it becomes a process of growth and change for the novelist himself. The writer seeks to hold onto his novel—because of the painful joy of creative work, with its continuity and uninterrupted purpose, and because he feels that what he has done can be made better but he longs to keep his ideal ever beyond reach.

THE WRITER'S ART is measured by the ability to transcend personal memory. Memory is the proof of life. Nothing really happens to a person unless it becomes memory. Some people pass through life in a state of total antisepsis. They have not touched life nor have they been touched by it. The artist-writer refines the ability of an individual to have contact with life, to be at one with others, to make their memories his own. In this sense, the writer widens the path to the subconscious.

THE QUESTION BEFORE US NOW is the ultimate form of human society—whether it will be permitted to continue disorganized and chaotic, leading almost inevitably to the same suicide that was the fate of other disorganized and chaotic groups in the past, or whether we can construct a necessary form of the whole. The job of writers is perhaps the hardest of all: They have to work with ideals.

A LIBRARY SYSTEM is more than a convenience for school children preparing for an examination. It is an index to the national health. It represents one of our vital resources. It is a powerful impetus for growth. It provides access to the future even more than it does to the past. It is a natural habitat for a functioning mind. It represents the headquarters for the endless process of education and learning that formal schooling can, in fact, only initiate. It is a diffusion center for the intellectual energy in the vital life of the mind. It is a seminal center for change. It is the delivery room of the intellect for people who like to bring ideas to life. It is also, or should be, a busy thoroughfare where a reasonably curious person can rub shoulders with the interesting and provocative people of history, and, indeed, where he or she can get on reading terms with some original ideas. It is an exchange center for basic facts, to be sure; but there is no reason why it should not fulfill Disraeli's description as a place which affords the consoling pleasures of the imagination.

SOME LIBRARIES HAVE OVERDONE the virtues of silence. Contemplation and chaos don't go together, but there is altogether too much restraint in libraries. A place comes alive when people can laugh out loud, when friends can discuss the things that concern them, and when other people can eavesdrop without too much straining. Keep the reading rooms sealed off, but make the rest of the library hospitable to the sound of the human voice. Bookshelves are not a final resting place for the written word; they are or should be the traffic centers for ideas—even when the traffic is noisy. The important thing is to get rid of the feeling that services for the dear departed are going on just across the hall.

I HAVE LEARNED to distrust speed reading and instant knowledge. Few joys of the mind can compare with the experience of lingering over deft character description, or hovering over a well-wrought passage. "Some people," said Alexander Pope, "will never learn anything . . . because they understand everything too soon."

CULTURE IS NOT JUST a dialogue between specialists and critics. It involves the whole magical process by which the human situation is sustained and advanced.

A POET, SAID ARISTOTLE, has the advantage of expressing the universal; the specialist expresses only the particular. The poet, moreover, can remind us that man's greatest energy comes not from his dynamos but from his dreams. The notion of where a man ought to be instead of where he is; the liberation from cramped prospects; the intimations of immortality through art—all these proceed naturally out of dreams. But the quality of a man's dreams can only be a reflection of his subconscious. What he puts into his subconscious, therefore, is quite literally the most important nourishment in the world.

A GOOD WRITER—OR ANY ARTIST, for that matter—is a prism for refracting beauty and truth. Human beings cannot live fully or joyously unless their sense of beauty is exercised and proclaimed. It is the writer's job to deal with these things of beauty in order to provide not necessarily a joy forever but a touch of loveliness that will last as long as society's capacity for beauty will last.

It is not necessarily true that the artist or writer has to be aloof or disdainful of the surrounding community. When the community itself has respect for the artist, when it develops a sense of responsibility towards the creative life, we will find that the artist will need no further inducement to become an actively proud and proudly active member of that community.

ART IS THE SUPREME MEANS for producing creative distortions—sometimes magnificent, sometimes terrifying—that can penetrate the false realities. Art is a system for living with unpredictables. Anyone who wants to pursue the great mysteries must be prepared to struggle with imponderables and take refuge in the imagination. "Let others wrangle, I will wonder," said Saint Augustine. Art is a way of getting through to the human subconscious, enabling people to have a greater sense of their uniqueness and fragility and preciousness than they can experience through any of the more systematic approaches.

ART—NATURALLY, INEVITABLY, INVARIABLY, IRREVOCABLY— begins in supreme abstractions. The end product, of course, can be the total opposite of the abstract; it may even deny the abstract. Even if and as it does so, however, it reflects its origins, which is as it should be. That is why it is absurd to ask the artist if he knows what he is doing. He may not in fact know what he is doing, but this is not relevant to the creative process. The monument to Vittorio Emmanuel in Rome may be one of the least abstract works on earth; it also happens to be one of the most terrifying rejections of the theory of grace ever to clog a municipal square. Even here, however, it is hard to believe there was not a wonderful moment or two during the original conception or execution of that appalling pile-up of stone when the designer didn't know what he was doing. I say this hope-fully. The severest thing that can be said about the monument is not that the designer didn't know what he was doing but that he did.

AN ARTIST, LIKE A PHILOSOPHER, may draw energy from what he does not know; the deeper his pursuit of the mysteries, the broader and more nourishing it becomes. And, like the scien-tist, he may find himself doing things without any clear idea of where he is going. But, as in both philosophy and science, what the artist doesn't know is no warrant for the celebration of ignorance, or for the annihilation of all tradition and the cumu-lative refinement of technique.

WE RECOGNIZE AND EXTOL the connection between the creative process and the quality of freedom—for the individual or the society. But we must be careful that virtues that exist only in proportion are not claimed *in extenso*. The artist who asserts the right not to know what he is doing must not suppose that all knowledge or craftsmanship are alien to the creative process. There is more to art than manifestations of pride in not know-ing. And there is more to becoming an artist than the individ-ual's assertion that he is one.

EXPERIMENTATION IN THE ARTS, always essential, has a natural ally in experience. And experience has something to say about the use of materials and craftsmanship in general. Departure from and even denial of tradition are supportable, but the obliteration of all tradition is chaos. True, there is always the possibility of finding splendor in chaos; but there may be better ways to arrive at it.

AT THE END OF THE CREATIVE PROCESS—after all the abstractions and abstracting, after all the communing with what is known or unknown, after all the sparks have flown across or fallen between the gaps—there comes a moment when what is done becomes separated from the artist and has a life of its own. Enter the critic, who has to determine whether that total creative process has come to anything.

THE CRITIC'S JOB by its very nature deprives him of the special dispensation enjoyed by the artist. Nowhere do the critic's credentials include the right not to know what he is doing. His criteria may be partially or even wholly abstract, but he has the obligation to define them. He is expected to state reasons—reasons to justify his analysis or his conclusions. His taste is subjective, but his critical standards have to be objective and explicable. It is an error to suppose that the critic should be completely devoid of history, or should have no interior knowledge of the demands of artistry and its attributes. What he deals with is not the claims or the effluvium of the artist but the work itself.

THE CRITIC CANNOT ACQUIESCE IN UNIFORMITY—even when it is staged in the name of essential freedom and experimentation. Revolutionary molds, if overly used or uncritically regarded, can become hideously unrevolutionary and trite. It was as a critic that Aristotle said that all art is imitation. An artist may regard this as a slur; if so, he is missing the point. The point is that the critic has to philosophize and develop perspective rather than just to scrutinize. Aristotle was thinking of first causes.

IT IS NOT TRUE that one picture is worth a thousand words. It takes only a few words—if they are the right words—to ignite the imagination and produce pictures in the mind far more focused and far more colorful than anything within the range of electronic communications.

THE ABILITY OF WORDS to throw a loop around human personality and to penetrate the inner space of character is exceeded by nothing that can be given visual form. Over the years, in numberless characterizations, attempts have been made to pictorialize Oscar Wilde's Dorian Gray, a depraved, debased, wanton, morally stagnant excuse for a man. Still, the visualization always falls short of the image created by the mind itself out of Wilde's words.

IF WE ARE LOOKING for a way to kill philosophy, then let us by all means put an end to print, for print is the natural habitat of ideas.

THERE IS A CURIOUS NOTION in some quarters that liberation is somehow to be equated not with freedom to create or to grow but with freedom to be an exhibitionist and narcissist. The result is not liberation but a vast depression. The outpourings of some shrunken and confused minds may be reflective of what is happening in our time, but they have very little to do with the enlargement of the human spirit, which is what liberation is all about.

THE FUNCTION OF THE CRITIC is not just to wage war against those who try to apply legal yardsticks to artistic expression but to fight against shabby merchandise masquerading as art. The fact that censorship is unworkable and evil doesn't mean that critics have to acquiesce to bilge or take leave of their senses and their sensitivities.

HONEST EXPERIMENTATION in the arts, always essential, is being seriously weakened by ignorance of or contempt for the past. An epidemic of imitativeness is enfeebling the development of necessary new techniques and perceptions. Shoddiness and ineptness are disguised as legitimate exercises in subjectivity or expressionism. The total result is hardly a triumph for creativity.

NOTHING REALLY HAPPENS TO A PERSON except as it is registered in the subconscious. This is where event and feeling become memory and where the proof of life is stored. The poet—and we use the term to include all those who have respect for and speak to the human spirit—can help to supply the subconscious with material to enhance its sensitivity, thus safeguarding it. The poet, too, can help to keep us from making ourselves over in the image of our electronic marvels. The danger is not so much that we will be controlled by the computer as that we may imitate it.

The poet reminds humans of their uniqueness. It is not necessary to possess the ultimate definition of this uniqueness. But even to speculate on it is a gain.

CREATIVE WRITING, said John Mason Brown, is the sweetest agony known to man. He is right. It is the one fatigue that produces inspiration, the exhaustion that exhilarates. Double-teaming the faculties of imagination and reasoning and keeping them coordinated and balanced is a tiring process, but there is something to show for your efforts. Socrates liked to refer to himself as a literary midwife—someone who helped to bring ideas to birth out of laboring minds. As a master of cerebral obstetrics, Socrates also knew and respected the conditions necessary for the conception of ideas.

BUYING A BOOK for public use involves choice. Removing it, banning it, or burning it attacks that choice. It makes pygmies of the burners and martyrs of the authors.

WHAT WILL CAUSE "EVERYMAN," who lives everywhere, who is preoccupied about different things and who lives under different systems, suddenly to find both unison and resonance in calling for safety and sense on earth? It is here that writers, especially novelists, poets, and playwrights, have their finest opportunity. If we have learned nothing else, it is that the ideas of the poets and artists penetrate where everything else has failed. The question, therefore, is not so much whether "Every-man" is capable of response, whatever his station, as whether there is someone to respond to.

HISTORY IN RETROSPECT is often a prime and vulnerable subject for criticism and caricature. The 1920s, for example, are frequently viewed as a world of rumrunners, spangled flappers, jazz, high-flying stocks, Teapot Domes, Gatsbys, Kennicotts, and Babbitts. But it was also a world that produced scholars and scientists who successfully challenged theories that had persisted for centuries; a world that was tooling up for great change; a world that was at least as interested in examining values as it was in experimenting with them; a world in which teachers such as Dewey, Kilpatrick, and Rugg were laying down new educational foundations; a world in which poets like A. E. Housman, W. B. Yeats, Robert Frost, Robinson Jeffers, and Edna St. Vincent Millay were finding responsive audiences; a world that relished the intellectual juxtaposition of George Bernard Shaw against H. G. Wells; a world that, for all its vaunted twitching, could sit still long enough to enjoy storytellers like Ellen Glasgow, Edith Wharton, Willa Cather, Thomas Hardy, Joseph Conrad, and E. M. Forster, and still notice new writers like Ernest Hemingway, Sinclair Lewis, and William Faulkner; a world which knew the enjoyment of laughter that men like Robert Benchley and Ring Lardner could provide.

THE BOOK IS STILL the finest portable university known to man.

IT IS DIFFICULT TO THINK of anything as truly modern as a book. Let us suppose that we lived in a world today without books—a world of total electronics in which all our communications were powered by transistors or by even more exotic power devices. Then let us suppose that someone suddenly came forward with a new communications invention. This invention would make the knowledge and experience of previous generations readily available to later generations. It would give people ready access to the ideas of the best minds. It could also light up the human brain with all sorts of wondrous and even joyous thoughts. The device would weigh no more than a pound or two and would be completely portable. It could also be owned by individuals at relatively low cost. The invention would be given the name "book." It would immediately be hailed as the greatest invention of the ages. It is only the fact that the device already exists that blinds us to its spectacular qualities.

A BOOK IS THE MOST varied product in the world. Its physical aspects are secondary to the range of thoughts and images it attempts to transfer to the mind of the reader. In this respect, a book is like a piece of rope; it takes on meaning only in connection with the things it holds together. What is carried by the book is nothing less than the life of the mind.

WHATEVER THE LIMITATIONS of a book, it is remarkably sound-proof, though it is beautifully audible to the inner ear. But the virtues of a good book transcend its silence. A good book is an adventure in sharing, but it is also an intensely personal experience. It offers fruitful solitude—sometimes in the heart of a crowd.

THERE IS A SIMPLE nonmedical technique for increasing longevity. This system goes by the name of "book." Through it, we can live hundreds of lifetimes in one. What is more, we can enjoy fabulous options. We can live in any age of our choosing. We can take possession of any experience. We can live inside the mind of any individual who has recorded an interesting thought, opened up new sluices of knowledge, engaged in depths of feeling or awareness beyond the scope of most mortals. This is what good books are all about.

A GOOD BOOK is a supple and yielding thing. It is meant to be argued with, challenged, marked up. It is a battleground for ideas and should show some evidence of a fight or at least some preliminary skirmishes. It is good for igniting minds. It is not the be-all and end-all of a balanced and productive life, but it can touch off needed thought and action.

THE BOOK IS NO SUBSTITUTE for experience. But neither is experience a substitute for the book. The growth of the human mind is still high adventure, in many ways the highest adventure on earth. And nothing is more characteristic of that growth than the transmission of vital thought and experience from one person to another and from one generation to another.

WHAT IS MOST ATTRACTIVE of all about a book is that it offers a life-giving transplantation—without anesthesia, all assertions by literary critics to the contrary notwithstanding. The transplantation of experience through books is no less vital than the transplantation of organs.

A BOOK IS NOT a fit subject for worship or enshrinement. It loses its charm and much of its value if accepted uncritically. No one would have been more disturbed than Aristotle if he could have known of the excessive and harmful veneration that would be accorded his ideas in centuries to come. Instead of using Aristotle as a powerful whetstone for sharpening the critical faculties in carving out even larger areas of knowledge, the early medieval scholars allowed their thinking to be dulled by literary ancestor worship.

A BOOK IS THE PARTICULARIZED ART of the writer. A book exercises yet replenishes the mind; it shatters the loneliness one feels in the group, yet it provides a splendid mutuality in isolation; it confronts the physical limitations of life yet seeks to transcend them; it helps a person to comprehend the need for stillness.

THE WRITER FULFILLS the greatest desire of human beings, which is to live beyond their own brief moment in time. The writer also makes it possible for the reader to establish lines of connection to previous lifetimes as well as lifetimes to come. The writer is a dispenser of options, providing freedom of choice: What kind of life does one wish to add to one's own?

WRITERS ARE SIMILAR to theologians in at least one respect. They seek to meet the hunger in humans for immortality. They make it possible for the reader to add many lifetimes to his own. The superior writer creates characters who live inside the reader. Good writers, therefore, are therapists. They provide a person with fruitful solitude—sometimes in the heart of a crowd. The writer gives us a chance to knit ourselves together.

THE PRIME FUNCTION of writers is to dig deep into their own times, to search for the root causes of crisis and give them a blazing clarity, to stretch the horizons of men's minds, and to evoke the natural greatness of men in response to great causes.

The real question is whether national greatness is ever possible without a great literature.

SO LONG AS PEOPLE value thought, there will be a central place for the written word. If we fail to succeed as writers, it will not be because we used the wrong medium but because we didn't have the right message.

THE WRITER, perhaps more than any of his fellow artists, has access to the human subconscious. His words sink deep, shaping dreams, easing the pain of loneliness, banishing incantations and omens, keeping alive the memories of the race, providing intimations of immortality, nourishing great anticipations, sharpening the instinct for justice, and imparting respect for the fragility of life. These functions are essential for human evolution. Without them, civilization becomes brittle and breaks easily. Society must be measured, therefore, not just by its display of power but by its attention to the conditions of creativity and its acceptance of human sovereignty as the highest value.

GOOD WRITING IS SOMETHING that begins in one's gizzard. An idea grows inside until it is ready. The process can be painful or satisfying or both, depending on the idea; but it is a process. We should suppose the function of the creative teacher is to encourage students to select their own subject from among the things that are coming to life in their minds. They will never learn to write well unless they develop the ability to dream and to be possessed by all sorts of notions that are itching to be expressed.

WHAT SHOULD CONCERN US is not the importance of society to the writer but the importance of the writer to society. The writer gives ideals to his time. He gives people a sense that what is necessary is also possible. And out of the writer's ideals a society discovers its reason for being.

WORDS ARE NOT TINS OF CHIPPED BEEF to be assembled at so many per minute. The significant thing about a sentence is not its brevity or its length but whether its message is conveyed with reasonable clarity and, if possible, style—difficult though it may be to define anything so amorphous as style. The surest way to destroy good writing is to have a clock ticking away in a man's mind who has been persuaded that speed reading is the key to good reading.

MOST OF THE GREAT ORDEALS in human history have produced great writers who acknowledged a special responsibility to their times. They defined the issues, recognized the values at stake, dramatized the nature of the challenge. In terms of today's needs, the challenge to writers is to see themselves as representatives of the human community. For the central issue facing the world today is not the state of this nation or that nation but the condition of man.

WHAT IS OFFENSIVE is not the use of coarse words, but the strained, artless, and unrelated nature of extraneous situations. Realism of this sort is about as appealing as an old goat emerging from a wet thicket.

IF THE LITERATURE OF PROTEST should disappear, our democracy will disappear along with it. Let other societies glorify themselves and preen in mirrors. Let others disparage or ban literature which is distasteful to the state. The good society thrives on criticism—however stilted or unfair it may be at times.

WRITING AS A CAREER is a good life and a rewarding one. Each book is a separate battle, requiring a skilled combination of strategy and tactics to accomplish a specific objective. It demands a mobilization of concentration—and concentration is or should be one of the higher gifts of human mental activity.

THE HUMAN MIND CRAVES FESTIVITY, diversion, and mirth. Nothing about an editor's job is more explicit or difficult than to find writers who know how to join words together in a way that pleases or excites the creative intelligence. Similarly, no challenge to the editor is more enduring than the need to help people take responsible pride in the evidence of human progress. And an editor's greatest satisfaction comes not when he is thanked for telling a reader something he doesn't know but when he is told that his journal has put into words something the reader instinctively feels.

EDITORS HAVE TO BE constantly on the prowl for new facts, new trends, new perceptions, new arenas. They have to recognize critical issues early enough to be able to sound an alert. They shouldn't have to wait until major events bulge into public view before taking notice. Nor need they fear going back for a second or third look; there may be odd pieces of history left lying around to be discerned, pieces that, when put together, may change the contours of an event, or at least our understanding of it.

IN OUR TIME, the creative mind is in jeopardy from half-formed ideas. The age seems to favor interruption and the staccato burst. But the writer of stature will find the eye of the hurricane. In that stillness, he will know his moment of triumph and he will create the words that will help to make us bigger than we are.

IT IS OFTEN ASKED whether America today can boast of writers who compare favorably with its writers in the first half of the twentieth century. Of course it can. Writers like William Styron, Kurt Vonnegut, Saul Bellow, Katherine Anne Porter, Joyce Carol Oates, Joseph Heller, and E. L. Doctorow, in the long perspective, will not suffer in comparison with Theodore Dreiser, John Dos Passos, John Steinbeck, Thomas Wolfe, Sinclair Lewis, Ellen Glasgow, and Edith Wharton. Is it fair to compare them with Faulkner and Hemingway? Perhaps not; some exceptions are inevitable. Comparisons aside, few writers can throw a neater loop around a time and mood than can William

Styron; few writers can illuminate the incongruous better than Kurt Vonnegut. The twentieth century as a whole has been a golden age for American literature.

Some vignettes of American writers we came to know in the early years of our editorship of the Saturday Review:

———————

WHO WAS HEMINGWAY'S GOD? He said his god painted wonderful pictures, wrote some fine books, fought Napoleon's rearguard actions in the retreat from Moscow, battled on both sides in the American Civil War, did away with yellow fever, taught Picasso how to draw and Jim Thorpe how to play football and Walter Johnson how to pitch (the ball was as small as a marble when it crossed the plate, and it would kill you if it hit you, but the Big Train never dusted anyone off, ever), sired Citation, and killed George Armstrong Custer. What did Hemingway think about Scott Fitzgerald's god? Clearly monotheistic. Hemingway said he was convinced that Scott's god was Irving Thalberg, the movie tycoon.

People spoke about his pugnaciousness, his worship of bullfighters and prizefighters, his fondness for rifles and big game—all of them were real enough but they were not the larger part. The larger part was his ability to see beneath surfaces and to enable others to do the same; his sensitivity to irony and paradox; his belief in the innate heroism of people or, at least, in their need for it. He was a lover not just of life but of language. He was an atrocious speller and had trouble with grammar, but he knew how to put words together so that they laid claim on the creative imagination. For all his literary honors, he was never sure of himself as a writer. He was miserable when he heard F. Scott Fitzgerald being praised. He liked to think of himself as Fitzgerald's mentor but for whom Scott's talents might never have fully matured. When he talked about Fitzgerald, it was always "Poor Scotty" this or "Poor Scotty" that. He tormented his wife Mary with his worries over financial insecurity even when his lawyer persisted in telling him his royalties guaranteed him lasting financial independence. These worries never left him. He was one of the three or four greatest writers—in any language—of his time. And a great writer, whatever his own inner agonies, is a prime resource of the human race. To enable people to live outside themselves is a gift beyond comparison.

WILLIAM FAULKNER DID MORE THAN to provide a literary portrait of a segment of the American South. He gave the South voice, pride, and spiritual nourishment, though many of the characters he brought to life in his novels were not distinguished for their spiritual dimensions. He was probably the greatest writer of his era and his growing recognition came at just the right time for a South that was seeking full restoration. He abhorred grandiosity. When he came to New York to revise his manuscripts and galley proofs, he would hole up in a little cubicle in the attic floor of the old 52nd Street mansion that went by the name of Random House. When I visited him in this New York setting he seemed strikingly out of place. Just outside his window were not magnolias but mammon and megalopolis. His voice was soft and tentative against the sharp, harsh sounds of the city. Physically, he was small to the point of seeming diminutive. He infused his writing with subtle gradations of color and textures that made much of his work elusive, almost surrealistic, at times. No one better exemplified Emily Dickinson's advice, "Tell it slant." He was supposed to be difficult to understand but the awareness and appreciation of him grew year by year. Outside the United States, literary critics who seemed uncertain about him for many years came to regard him as the finest American writer of his time. What made this evaluation all the more striking was that their earlier judgment favored Hemingway, of whom Faulkner in many ways was the quintessential opposite. The juxtaposition, whether of style or person, couldn't have been more striking. The bullfight arena versus the soft-scented Southern garden. The long stride versus the quiet, short steps. The open brawl versus the smoldering hurt. Dynamite versus lace. Some of the critics abroad were perplexed by the differences but it told them a great deal about a society that could produce both authors.

SINCLAIR LEWIS: Tall, skinny, angular. When he bent forward to scrutinize you, he had the aspect of a praying mantis on his hind legs. He won all the accolades the critics and the prize-givers, including the Nobel jury, had to offer. He had everything as a writer except sustaining power. The ultimate jury—people who buy and read books—never really fell in love with him. They bought his new stories but had no passion to read them a second time. Why? His characters were sharply drawn and often they had a point to make but most of them seemed too flimsy to be totally convincing; they seemed to reflect an incomplete, grudging notion of what the human species in America was really like. However pointed his descriptions, the total picture seemed somewhat out of focus. For writers to be truly great, their books must be re-discovered, re-read, and speak to an eternal and universal quality in the race. Perhaps his time will come again. As of now, his time is yesterday.

THE BOOK PUBLIC as a whole had the erroneous impression that John Steinbeck was aloof and even diffident; but he loved good company, just so long as it was not too large. He loved to travel and to meet with fellow writers in different parts of the world. I found him genuinely shy, extremely reluctant to get into public debate but deeply concerned and even agitated over public issues. He was hesitant to talk about his own books. First and foremost, he was a masterful storyteller and a creator of character. Critics have debated whether Steinbeck or Dos Passos was the great American depression novelist. The argument is pointless. Each described a different segment of America. Steinbeck's canvas was open country—California and the American Southwest. Dos Passos wrote mostly about intellectuals or pseudo-intellectuals in the Eastern big cities. Steinbeck's people were non-ideological types—oddballs, human rejects, wayfarers, hangers-on, many of them; but they were warm and real and were caught up in situations that baffled but excited the imagination. They were all part of an America that never lost its youth or friendliness or frailty.

OSCAR HAMMERSTEIN was totally without ambiguity or circumspection. He never hesitated to make unequivocal alliances—

with causes or human beings. He was deeply caught up in the main currents of his time. He was endlessly creative, instinctively friendly and trusting. He believed in children, sunny mornings, love at first sight, happy surprises, good humor, good deeds, golden wheat fields, and flaming sunsets. He had no interest in the cheap sex and casual violence that were the thematic staples of some of his contemporaries. He unabashedly extolled the essential decency of people and never got tired of lyricizing their capacity to extricate themselves from absurd and painful situations. For a long time—especially during the first two decades of his career—the drama critics flayed him because they thought him too sentimental, too addicted to what they regarded as implausible triumphs over bleak realities. Eventually, however, almost all of them came to sing his praises along with his songs. Even the toughest of them had to admit they felt better about belonging to the human species after spending an evening with Rodgers and Hammerstein.

REX STOUT had a wide circle of friends. He teased them unmercifully, gave them a rough time in political discussions, loved them all with openness and ebullience. If I argued with him about politics, I could almost feel the thunder build up inside him. When it reached a point where it could no longer be contained, out would come, "The hell you say!" If there were hills around, the sound would boom and echo through the valleys. And then he would suddenly turn soft and grin and suggest a game of chess. Like many other artists, he was a fascinating assortment of contrasts. He was a banker turned mystery-story writer, an expert on fine wines and foods who was one of the most passionate anti-Nazis of his time, a lover of games who was among the leaders of the world government movement. In any company, his voice was the most resonant, especially if the subject was human freedom. No mystery-story writer was more ingenious in polishing off people in his tales—or more adept at involving them in absurd situations. But he was a family man first and foremost and delighted in the placid country life.

ONCE, AT A DODGER BASEBALL GAME in Los Angeles, I asked Will Durant if he was 94 or 95. "Ninety-four," he shot back. "You don't think I'd be doing anything as foolish as this if I were 95, do you? I'd be home working." Few worked harder at writing than he did. With his wife, Ariel, he produced a vast opus on the history of civilization. Ariel described the quintessence of her husband's approach to history when she said, "Will often talked of historical characters as more real than the vanishing figures and events of the day; Luther, Erasmus, Calvin, Henry VIII, Gutenberg, Rabelais, and Copernicus were more vital, more lasting in their influence, than the politics, prizefights, murders, fashions, market reports, and baseball scores of the daily press. So we buried our heads in the living past rather than the dying present."

Critics no longer put down the Durants on the ground of inadequate scholarship. On the contrary: The Durants are hailed because they have introduced large numbers of readers to the historical procession. They have been more attracted to history's pageantry, perhaps, than to its imponderables, but they have not detached themselves from the search for meaning. They have made important connections between people and events not merely within each era but in the long perspective of history. Whether they were writing about philosophy or civilization, they were always aware that history's effects are felt far beyond the causal arena. They made no pretense of being definitive; they regarded themselves rather as synthesizers. As such, they belong to a rare breed.

ROBERT E. SHERWOOD was as tall and trim as a poplar and as gentle as a soft breeze. He had been brought up—as had most history-conscious young men of his generation—with the notion that the way to avert war was to spurn it. He was awakened by the Hitlerian realities. He put his dramatic skills to work in helping to define the issues for his fellow Americans. He had a highly developed sense of history; he was mindful of present dangers but was also captured by the vision of a world congenial to the quest for human perfectibility. As a playwright, he never trifled with people's hopes. He gave them good reason for believing in themselves. Sherwood was one of the first writers to perceive that the consequences of events in Europe in the late thirties extended to the whole of the human race. He knew that the Second World War was a crucible for the future. If his thinking about America's role in world affairs changed from what it had been in the early years following the First World War, it was largely because he realized that the whole of humanity was involved.

BUCKY FULLER very early discovered the secret of perpetual curiosity and spent all his life trying to give the secret away. Of all his attributes, none was more compelling than his ability to transmit to others his love for the cosmos and everything that went with it. The good will that radiated from him, his enthusiasm for new directions and new options, his capacity for liberating the human imagination from earthbound concepts and for propelling human beings into a new relationship with the universe—all this lit up the minds of his friends, auditors, and readers. The affection of students for Bucky Fuller offered the strongest possible evidence that young people are responsive to the values that give affirmative energy to a society. People would listen to him for hours even though they might not understand very much of what he was saying. What they did understand through him, however, was that the main end of science was not to answer questions but to generate new ones; not to relieve curiosity but to enlarge it and ignite it; not to build better machines but to enable people to know how to run them and control them. I have known very few people who came away from a lecture by Bucky who did not forever after have an enhanced sense of sublime wonder when looking at a starlit sky.

NO EDITORIALIST WRITING about the human condition in our time had more to say about deprivation or suffering than Margaret Bourke-White through her photographs. And few philosophers or dramatists penetrated more deeply into the wondrous possibilities of human hopefulness and dignity. She had a gift for laughter and joyousness. Even when stricken with a crippling disease, she pursued the arts of friendship. She amazed her doctors by continuing with her photography assignments despite her infirmity. They knew that no medicine or surgery they might provide was as powerful as her own determination to function fully and independently. She paid little attention to the technological advances that revolutionized photography. Her sensitivity to light and shadow was so exquisitely developed that she didn't have to use light meters. She always traveled the shortest distance between her subject and the shutter. She never regarded herself as a great photographer, but she was a relentless perfectionist with her own work. The love she lavished on her photography was a very real reflection of her love for people and for the nobility of life itself. From her I learned to respect the human capacity for converting hope into life-giving purpose.

No remembrances of literary people in this book would be complete without the gifted group who founded or were associated with the Saturday Review of Literature *in its early years. Working with them was probably the greatest privilege of my life.*

HENRY SEIDEL CANBY, FOUNDING EDITOR of the *Saturday Review of Literature,* set the judicious, authoritative tone for the magazine in his own writings. He presided over the staff with calm, certainty of purpose, and unquestioned good will. As a critic, he never denounced; he merely registered a dispassionate and documented disapproval. A book review to him was not a basin for depositing personal frustrations or a stage for exhibiting knowledge superior to the author's. The critic's job, as he saw it, was to bring good taste and trained intelligence to bear on the evaluation of a book as an essential public service. Under Canby, the *Saturday Review* won acclaim for the excellence of its essays and reviews. But the publishing of a literary journal called for more than seasoned intellectual judgments. The editor had to be a survival specialist in an arena of cold-turkey creditors and humorless auditors. And Henry Canby had no particular gift for business problems. Physically, he appeared unreasonably unprepossessing and underproportioned. But he had extraordinary persistence and staying power. "Literature," he wrote, "is wonderfully adapted to be the sensitive film upon which change is recorded. The books of this century have been only shadows of reality, but they have been prophetic shadows running ahead of the rising sun. And the noting and the interpreting of these areas of humanity have been the service to which the *Saturday Review* has been dedicated."

AMY LOVEMAN, ONE OF THE FOUNDERS of the *Saturday Review of Literature,* had no patience with the cynicism that went in and out of fashion; she thought nothing was more wasteful than defeatism—whether in literature or in life. This large view never left her. How many books she had to handle and read for the *Saturday Review* and Book-of-the-Month Club she herself never dared to guess. But now and then she would come across something of quality and her reward could not have been more complete if she had discovered an unpublished novel by Jane Austen. It is doubtful, however, whether anything gave her greater satisfaction than working with new writers. Her advice was precise, crisp, practical, built on a solid foundation of reasonable explanation. And underlying everything else was an almost epic kindness. She was less cluttered emotionally than any person I have ever known. Her horizons were unblurred by petty assertions or a sovereign ego. Her concerns pointed outward, and that outlook carried over to others. I can't recall ever hearing a petty argument in her presence or a single instance when people did not respond to her presence by liberating themselves from trivia. Her nobility was a universe; and to know it was to soar inside it.

GEORGE STEVENS WAS EDITOR-IN-CHIEF of the *Saturday Review of Literature* in the 1930s and my immediate predecessor. He and Amy Loveman were the valiant duo who did practically all the work—assigning books for review, editing the copy, making up the magazine, and seeing it through the printers. Keeping a literary journal alive during those depression years was a high wire act, and I've always admired George for his generalship at a difficult time. He left *Saturday Review* in 1940 to become editor of J. P. Lippincott, where his editorial craftsmanship and literary interests were in abundant evidence until his retirement in 1975. George was an editor's editor. He was able to make sound judgments on every phase of book publishing, from editorial policy and selection to anticipation of the changing needs of the literary marketplace. He had highly developed enthusiasms, as was reflected by his partiality to writers like Ellen Glasgow, Edith Wharton, Joseph Conrad, and John Steinbeck. His continuing encouragement to me over the years meant far more to me than I think he realized. Our meetings were not frequent but they were steady. He was a man of strong but well-rounded tastes whose broad knowledge—from literature and politics to music and baseball—made conversation a delight.

WILLIAM ROSE BENÉT, associate editor of the *Saturday Review of Literature* at its birth, stayed close to his poetry and his Phoenix Nest column; but in his restrained, patient way he made a religion out of believing in people and helping them. "He is a man of mingled fire and honey," wrote Dr. Canby, "whose concern is every human interest but his own." No one in the United States did more to encourage poets of all ages. He would suffer visibly whenever he had to write a note of rejection, especially when a poetry submission was accompanied by a letter showing the writer to be a person of high hopes. His supporters never wavered in their admiration of his abilities as a poetry editor, and they gave high honors to his own poetry as well. When Don Marquis reviewed Benét's *Moons of Grandeur* for the old *New York Sun* he wrote, "Was Benét ever in Italy? No matter . . . he has Italy in him. Italy and Egypt and every other country that was ever warmed by the sun of beauty. There are very few people writing verse who have the power to charm us and enchant us away with them as Benét can. He has found the horse with wings."

CHRISTOPHER MORLEY brought a quality of sagacious merriment and controlled omniscience to the American literary scene. Few American essayists of his time had greater energy or inventiveness. Almost none knew better the beautiful distinction between humor and wit. Scarcely a leaf turned in the universe without its causing some felicitous thought to come to life in his mind, fortified by the enriching and apt allusion. It was natural that he should have been the editor of *Bartlett's Familiar Quota-*

tions. He was the kind of man who would go to the end of the world for moment of creative splendor. He was not the easiest person to get along with. He could make personal fancy seem like a towering test of principle. He could be caustic, prickly, petulant. But all this became inconsequential alongside his charm, his laughter, and his readiness to do handsprings for a good book. Among his favorite quotations was a line in a letter from Keats to Reynolds: "Now it appears to me that almost any man may, like the spider, spin from his own innards his own airy Citadel." Christopher Morley was such a man; his Citadel had the kind of crisp airiness that freshened other minds and kept forever new wonderful respect for the creative imagination.

BERNARD DE VOTO, who succeeded Henry Seidel Canby as editor of *Saturday Review,* was as open and gutsy as the Utah town of his childhood. Whether in his writing style or in his person, he was primed for instant combat. If he indulged himself in literary overkill or sometimes went after inappropriate targets, he commanded respect for his devotion to the written word and for his defense of the place of the book in our society. He was a passionate advocate of the American pioneering tradition. The *Saturday Review* gave Benny DeVoto ample scope for literary crusading and controversy. Among those he growled at were Van Wyck Brooks, Lewis Mumford, Harold Stearns, Ezra Pound, T. S. Eliot, Malcolm Cowley, Edmund Wilson, Granville Hicks, Emma Goldman, Mike Gold. Among those who growled back were Edmund Wilson and Sinclair Lewis. Were the others silent because they didn't take him seriously? Was it because he was such a militant antagonist of censorship and violation of human rights that his tilting at literary contemporaries could be accommodated as part of the allowable margin for error accorded critics of worth? Or was it that he had a germ of truth that few wished to debate—the truth that too much of our literature was detached from its native soil and was therefore lacking in essential nutrients?

EVERYTHING ABOUT BENNETT CERF, who served as *Saturday Review*'s Contributing Editor for about fifteen years, made an imprint on those who knew him—his utter lack of circumspection about the things he liked or disliked; his almost supernatural gift for making friends and keeping them stocked with books or goodies of one sort or another; his cascading anecdotes and horrendous puns; his talent for being equally at home with bibliophiles, burlesque queens, academicians, Hollywood luminaries, poets, business tycoons, scientists, quarterbacks, spacemen, and literary critics. He appropriated stories from others; to him, the unforgivable offense was not in stealing a story but in telling it poorly. He was so obvious about his thefts that he was honest. "The thing you've got to know about me is that I'm a ham," he would say—and he meant it. But all the joyousness, excitement, and fireworks associated with his name should not be allowed to obscure his main aim and achievement in life. He set out to be a book publisher, and he became one of the very best.

IT REQUIRES THE DESCRIPTIVE POWERS of one of the old Russian literary masters to do justice to J. R. Cominsky, publisher of *Saturday Review* from 1942 to 1968. Jack's special qualities were explicit and pronounced to the point of being phenomenal. If enthusiasm is the natural enemy of fatigue, Jack was in a perpetual condition of rejuvenation. Given a problem with nine parts marked impossible and one part possible, he had no difficulty in inverting the equation and making it work. He carried a workload that was the despair and disbelief of his colleagues. His checklist of things to be done kept filling up like rain barrels during a monsoon. The most important thing Jack did for *Saturday Review* was to force us to look ahead. He got us moving in the direction of our dreams. A few weeks before he died, Jack was in my office when a visitor was commenting on the fact that *Saturday Review*'s readership had grown to sixhundred thousand from the fifteen thousand when JRC came to *Saturday Review*. Jack looked at me and winked. "We're just getting started," he said. This spirit of renewal was his greatest legacy to *Saturday Review*.

JOHN MASON BROWN, *Saturday Review*'s Associate Editor and drama critic, turned his creativity in many directions, but his main bent was the theatre; he was probably its leading authority and certainly its best friend. He had few peers as a critic and none as a public speaker. I knew of no contemporary dramatic reviewer who had a greater gift for the felicitous use of the English language. The pictures he painted in the listener's mind had far greater substance and color than those the eye alone could perceive. His writings progressively widened until they embraced the world and, indeed, the arena of events and ideas. He made full use of the unique advantages of magazine journalism to combine topical material with the literary and the historical. His truly majestic study of Robert E. Sherwood, playwright, author, advisor to presidents, provided his readers with a lasting picture of a man who both dramatized history and made it. The sense of perennial discovery was the main characteristic of John Brown and his work. This and the fact that he knew the value of joy.

ONE OF THE MOST REMARKABLE MEN I have ever known was, by profession, a petroleum geologist—Everette Lee DeGolyer. He had more sides to him than an exhibit of mobiles—all of them authentic. He was best known for his spectacular oil discoveries and as a pioneer and leader in his field. To other oil men he was a legend. Not so well known, however, was the nature of the man himself. In one setting he was a cool, dispassionate, analytical scientist-historian; in another, a warmly compassionate man who could be moved to tears by a sentimental play. Or, he could be the indefatigable researcher, relentlessly pursuing an obscure fact, or taking abiding delight in a book discovery, or in working on a sentence until it turned just right, or in conversations with friends and cronies that might mix abstract ideas, earthy illustrations, scientific data, random speculation, and droll stories. From Mr. De, a political conservative, I learned a lot about genuine liberalism and the largeness of the human spirit. Before he died, he told me that the success of the *Saturday Review of Literature,* following its early struggle to stay alive, delighted him as much if not more than his biggest oil strike. Yet he ultimately transferred his ownership of the magazine to those of us responsible for its publication, never having taken a cent himself from the enterprise. Mr. De the legend and Mr. De the man properly belong to his own collection of Americana.

9

Healing and Belief

OVER THE YEARS, medical science has identified the primary systems of the human body—circulatory system, digestive system, endocrine system, autonomic nervous system, parasympathetic nervous system, and the immune system. But two other systems that are central in the proper functioning of a human being need to be emphasized: the healing system and the belief system. The two work together. The healing system is the way the body mobilizes all its resources to combat disease. The belief system is often the activator of the healing system. The belief system represents the unique element in human beings that makes it possible for the human mind to affect the workings of the body. How one responds—intellectually, emotionally, or spiritually—to one's problems has a great deal to do with the way the human body functions. One's confidence, or lack of it, in the prospects of recovery from serious illness affects the chemistry of the body. The belief system converts hope, robust expectations, and the will to live into plus factors in any contest of forces involving disease. The belief system is no substitute for competent medical attention in serious illness or vice versa. Both are essential. The belief system is not just a state of mind. It is a prime physiological reality. It is the application of options to the maintenance of health and the fight against disease. It is the master switch that gets the most out of whatever is possible. The greatest force in the human body is the natural drive of the body to heal itself—but that force is not independent of the belief system, which can translate expectations into physiological change. Nothing is more wonderous about the fifteen billion neurons in the human brain than their ability to convert thoughts, hopes, ideas, and attitudes into chemical substances. Everything begins, therefore, with belief. What we believe is the most powerful option of all.

CONSIDERING THE NUMBER of different species on this planet, the chances of being born a human being are about one in two billion. Considering the number of sperm produced by a single mating experience, the particular sperm that resulted in you was one in several million, at least. What is most astounding of all, however, is the absence of human awareness over the phenomenal triumph over impossible odds that a single human being represents. Human beings have been able to comprehend everything in the world except their uniqueness. Perhaps it is just as well. If ever we begin to contemplate our own composite wonder, we will lose ourselves in celebration and have time for nothing else.

WE MAY NOT BE ABLE to unravel the ultimate mystery of life but one thing is certainly within our capacity: We can do a better job of caring for human life than we are now doing.

SCIENCE AND COMMON SENSE converge in the ultimate mission of human intelligence—the full potentiation of the individual. This process is not confined to the development of human abilities. It involves in equal measure the way human beings ward off breakdown and cope with it when it occurs. It has to do with the will to live and the physiological benefits of creativity and the positive emotions. It assigns proper value to hope, faith, laughter, and confidence in the life force.

THE HUMAN HEALING SYSTEM has been beautifully honed by three million years of evolution in coping not just with its disorders but with detours, deflections, and errors.

ONE OF THE MAIN FUNCTIONS of the doctor is to engage to the fullest the patient's own ability to mobilize the forces of mind and body in turning back disease.

THE ART OF HEALING is still a frontier profession.

FRANCIS W. PEABODY, in his remarkable little volume, *The Care of the Patient,* described a case in which the hospital staff

... was contented with a half-truth. The investigation of [the] patient was decidedly unscientific in that it stopped short of even an attempt to determine the real cause of the symptoms. As soon as organic disease could be excluded, the whole problem was given up, but the symptoms persisted. The case was a medical failure in note of the fact that the patient went home with the assurance that there was "nothing the matter with her."

This fact—that a patient, according to standard diagnostic procedures, may not be ill—is secondary to the patient's cry for help. If a doctor cannot hear this cry above the electronic chatter of his technological armamentarium, he is not meeting the main need being put before him.

THE ART OF THE DOCTOR is to convey the possibilities of the human healing system to individuals who are conditioned to thinking of illness mainly in terms of bugs, pains, mysterious growths, infection, inflammations, prescriptions, and hospital beds. This is one reason why the goal of medical education should be to produce men and women who are not just well trained but well educated.

THE *Annals of Internal Medicine* FOR NOVEMBER 1938 reviewed the importance of the patient's faith in the physician as a significant factor in overcoming disease. The main point that emerged from this paper was that the patient's belief in the healing power of the physician is often more important than the treatment itself in reversing the course of an illness. Dr. A. K. Shapiro has documented in his various studies ("A Contribution to a History of the Placebo Effect," *Behavioral Sciences*, 1960, and "Attitudes Toward the Use of Placebos in Treatment," *The Journal of Nervous and Mental Diseases*, (1960) the fact that what the patient expects to happen as the result of a relationship with a physician can be as potent in touching off biochemical processes as any medication—or any placebo, for that matter.

THE PHYSICIAN MUST SUPPLY not just the scientific competence but the spiritual nourishment that his patients need. The most potent medicine available to the physician is the confidence placed in him by the patient. The next most potent medicine is the physician's ability to harness the natural drive of the human body and mind to overcome its maladies.

SIR WILLIAM OSLER, the celebrated clinician, advised medical students to forego feelings of cynicism about faith. He would review for his students the various methods used by medical science in the treatment of patients over the years—all the way from applications of dung to the removal of blood—and then remind them that it was a tribute to the durability of the human species that it was able to survive such ministrations.

THE QUINTESSENCE OF HUMAN UNIQUENESS is represented by the ability of the human brain to comprehend, or try to comprehend, its own inner workings and to exercise a significant measure of control over those inner workings through thought. The reason human beings will continue to evolve is that they can make ever more complex connections between their desires and their destinies, between their expectations and their actions. And as they learn more about the way their thoughts and attitudes affect their internal chemistry, they will discover the greatest factor in their own evolution—the governance of their own totalities.

PATIENTS TEND TO MOVE in the direction of their hopes or fears. If they have strong confidence in themselves and their physicians, they tend to have a better outcome than if they are morose and defeatist. A paper in *Lancet* by S. Greer, T. Morris, and K. W. Pettingale (October 13, 1979) reported that a study of sixty-nine breast cancer cases showed that the psychological response of the patients was a significant factor in the course of the disease. Those patients who "had a fighting spirit" and who wouldn't accept a negative verdict were far more likely to improve than those who responded with "stoic acceptance of feelings of helplessness and hopelessness."

IT MAKES NO SENSE to believe that only the negative emotions have an effect on the body's chemistry. Every emotion, negative or positive, makes its registrations on the body's systems.

COMPETENT OBSERVERS have written about yogis in India who were trained to slow down their pulses to a few beats per minute, or who can order their skin to resist burning from hot surfaces. But systematic scrutiny of such phenomena has lagged behind popular interest, the result being that the entire field has been colored by guesswork and extraordinary claims. Out of it all, however, has emerged the undeniable evidence that the human mind can be trained to play an important part both in preventing disease and in overcoming it when it occurs. The entire biofeedback movement has gained in stature as the result of such new research. In any case, many members of the medical profession are pressing for greater emphasis on mind-body interactions and the attack on illness.

THE HUMAN BODY experiences a powerful gravitational pull in the direction of hope. That is why the patient's hopes are the physician's secret weapon. They are the hidden ingredient in any prescription. The physician will do everything he can, therefore, to bolster attitudes, nourish the outlook on life, and encourage confidence in the patient.

WE MUST LEARN never to underestimate the capacity of the human mind and body to regenerate—even when the prospects seem most wretched. The life-force may be the least understood force on earth. William James said that human beings tend to live too far within self-imposed limits. It is possible that these limits will recede when we respect more fully the natural drive of the human mind and body toward perfectibility and regeneration. Protecting and cherishing that natural drive may well represent the finest exercise of human freedom.

PEOPLE SEE OR READ ABOUT PERSONS—not just yogis—whose minds can cope with pain or can control bleeding, and there is a gee-whiz reaction akin to what happens when people see bears ride bicycles or when they see a woman sawed in half at the circus. Yet nothing in the field of vended magic is as arresting as new knowledge about the regulatory possibilities of the mind. A new frontier in the understanding of life is being opened up. It represents one of the main challenges confronting medical science. We need to know more about the workings of the human mind—how endorphins are manufactured and activated; how norepinephrine and serotonin interact with each other and with other chemicals in creating thought-processes; how messages from the brain are transmitted by way of the hypothalamus into the endocrine system; how the conscious intelligence produces beta waves and what functions are carried out by those waves both in activating the mind and in governing the body; and how electrical fields are created by brain energy.

THE FACT THAT CANCER is an extreme form of human disease does not mean that all established principles for combatting illness cease to have validity. One of these principles holds that even as disease is attacked the patient must be bolstered in every way. Indeed, the more drastic the treatment, the more important it becomes to fortify and put to work the individual's own resources—a healthy life style, a robust will to live, a determination to make the most out of whatever is possible. These are intangibles, to be sure, but intangibles define a human being. They also have something to do with the connection between the belief system and the healing system—or the translation of purpose into physiological reality. Most important of all perhaps is the fact that intangibles help set a stage for the optimum use of medical science.

THE KIND OF LIFE LIVED BY a patient under conditions of vigorous response to a challenge is infinitely preferable to a crunching, desperate winding-down.

THE WILL TO LIVE is a window on the future. It opens the individual to such help as the outside world has to offer, and it connects that help to the body's own capability for fighting disease. It enables the human body to make the most of itself. It is not a theoretical abstraction but a physiologic reality with therapeutic characteristics.

THE UNBEARABLE TRAGEDY is not death but dying in an alien arena—separated from dignity, separated from the warmth of familiar things, separated from the ever-present ministrations of a loving relationship and an outstretched hand.

THE DOCTOR'S RESPECT FOR LIFE, his special qualities of compassion and tenderness—even under the most devilish of circumstances—these are the vital ingredients of his art.

PEOPLE WHO ARE SERIOUSLY ILL need to believe that they have a chance. They respond not just to the doctor's attitude but to the mood of the people very close to them. If hope is missing from the eyes and from the voices of their families, the absence will be felt. If only in terms of the ricochet effect on his patient, should the physician not treat the entire family?

ABOUT HALF THE PEOPLE who have heart attacks never make it to the hospital. An important contributing reason is that the panic that accompanies the attack constricts the blood vessels and imposes an additional and sometimes intolerable burden on the heart. If I could be granted just one wish in the war against disease, it would be to liberate people from the panic that is the almost instinctive response to the fact of serious illness. Illness and panic are in a state of ominous interaction. Panic adds acute stress to existing disease. It puts an additional drain on the adrenal glands and on the endocrine system in general. It creates an environment conducive to illness and antagonistic to treatment.

PANIC AND THE WILL TO LIVE are natural enemies. Hope and the will to live are the best antidotes to panic. They fortify the healing system. The responsible physician does not purvey panic, whatever his obligations to the truth. The responsible physician engages the patient's will to live. Truth can be communicated with moral artistry or it can be dumped on a patient like a truckload of bricks.

THE PHYSICIAN'S METHOD of delivering truth to a patient can help combat or help intensify disease. If delivered the wrong way, the truth can produce panic and erode hope—a dismal state that hardly offers an ideal environment for making the most of the physician's ministrations. If delivered the right way, however, the truth can bolster the patient's will to live, and various plus factors can come into play.

THE TREATMENT OF A PATIENT is incomplete if it is confined to diagnosis and the administration of medicines or other procedures. It becomes complete only when the patient's own resources and capacities are fully engaged. This is where the science of medicine and the art of medicine come together.

WHAT IS THE MOST PAINFUL and devastating question that can be asked about modern medical practice? It is not whether most physicians are up to date in their knowledge or in their techniques but whether too many of them know more about disease than about the person in whom the disease exists.

THE MODERN PHYSICIAN strides forth into the world from medical school with a certificate of learning in one hand and a vast array of exotic medications and technological devices in the other. But the humans who look to him for help are fragile, perplexed, vulnerable. More than anything else, they want to know that they matter. They don't want anything to come between them and their physicians—not an electronic device or even a nurse's interruption. People want their physicians to be finely tuned human beings capable of exquisite sensitivity and tenderness. Patients do not warm up to impersonal and detached super-scientists. They want to feel that the doctor who is examining them is thinking of nothing else. If his telephone rings, they feel a break in the circuit and are pained.

THE WISE PHYSICIAN makes a careful estimate of the emotional needs of the patient. He creates a mood of confidence for the encounter with diagnostic technology. He explains that he will not attach sovereign importance to the results. He doesn't abandon the patient to a device if he can possibly help it. The wise physician understands, too, that the patient's biochemistry may respond differently to a stress challenge under circumstances of anxiety than under circumstances of physical strain.

THE CHANCES OF A PATIENT opposing or resenting medical technology are in direct proportion to the distance of the physician from the scene. People feel secure in the presence of their doctors. It is only when the patients are dispatched to other places and are deprived of direct contact with or access to their physician that they tend to become uneasy. And the more they are removed from the main source of their security, the more apprehensive they become.

IS NO PENALTY TO BE ATTACHED TO a process in which a human being feels less important than the illness being diagnosed and treated? Is there nothing upsetting or even terrifying about being made to run a gauntlet of different diagnostic faces, different instrumentations, and different procedures at a time when the last thing in the world a patient needs is more uncertainty? The medical technologist celebrates computerized tomography. The patient celebrates the outstretched hand.

THE INTENSIVE CARE UNIT is where we find the grand assembly of medical invention. Technically, it does everything expected of it. It monitors the patient and picks up even the most obscure hint of biological failure. Yet the crisis atmosphere it produces contributes very little to the patient's peace of mind at a critical time. Every blip and clink remind the patient that he or she is in a precarious condition. If panic is to be avoided at all costs, the intensive care unit can hardly be considered a bargain. It is as omnipresent as it is efficient; as forbidding as it is ingenious.

THE MORE EXOTIC and sophisticated the technology, the greater the likelihood that patients will feel diminished or apprehensive. The physician who cannot afford the time to stay close to the patient during this experience had better find effective equivalents, for the ultimate effect of those tests can be harmful psychologically and therefore physiologically. Patients cannot be blamed for retreating from experiences they find distasteful or upsetting. The argument that the procedures are necessary for the patient's own good misses the point, for the source of the patient's disquiet is not the procedure itself so much as the climate or the context in which it occurs. The absence of human warmth during those experiences tends to figure larger in the reactions of patients than the vaunted value of the tests.

MEDICAL TECHNOLOGY has clearly justified its existence on any balance sheet of performance and problems. But the problems are not minor. They affect the health and well-being of the patient. What is most significant about these problems is that they are all manageable.

THE PRACTICE OF MEDICINE, as has been emphasized over the centuries by almost every great medical teacher (from Hippocrates to Holmes, from Galen to Cannon, from Castiglione to Osler), calls first of all for a deeply human response by the physician to the cry of the patient for help. In the overwhelming majority of cases, as Franz Ingelfinger, the late and much-beloved editor of the *New England Journal of Medicine* pointed out, what patients need most of all is assurance that their own healing systems are beautifully designed to handle most of their complaints. The physician who understands the importance of sitting at the bedside, even though his presence may actually be in the nature of a placebo equivalent, is attending to a prevalent and quintessential need.

THE OVERRIDING ISSUE before medicine today is one not of proficiency but of humanity. No one can any longer doubt the ability of medical technologists to devise the electronic equipment that makes precise calibrations that can pick up the slightest variation in the sodium-potassium exchange or the amount of energy transmitted to the human heart. But what about the extent to which foreboding or even panic engendered by those same electronic marvels can add to the disorder being calibrated? The poets used to tell us that man is the measure of all things. Are we now to believe that measures come ahead of men?

MEDICAL SCIENCE MAY CHANGE, but the need to understand and deal with human beings remains constant. Nothing is more important in medical education, therefore, than "reverence for life," to use Schweitzer's phrase. Moral values, an important aspect of human uniqueness, are not perishable or evanescent or replaceable. So long as the physician gives emphasis to the supreme importance of human individuality and to his own ability to earn and keep the confidence of the human beings who look to him for vital answers—so long as he can do this, he can consider himself an artist and a philosopher.

THE MOST COSTLY DISEASE IN AMERICA is not cancer or coronaries. The most costly disease is boredom—costly for both individual and society.

LONGEVITY BY ITSELF is indistinguishable from vegetation. A man can acquire a new pancreas, kidney, liver, heart, bone marrow, and lung, but he will succumb to boredom if his mind is without a horizon.

THE WAR AGAINST MICROBES has been largely won, but the struggle for equanimity is being lost. It is not just the congestion outside us—a congestion of people and ideas and issues—but our inner congestion that is hurting us. Our experiences come at us in such profusion and from so many different directions that they are never really sorted out, much less absorbed. The result is clutter and confusion. We gorge the senses and starve the sensitivities.

"YOUR HEALTH IS BOUND TO BE AFFECTED," Boris Pasternak wrote in *Dr. Zhivago*, "if, day after day, you say the opposite of what you feel, if you grovel before what you dislike and rejoice at what brings you nothing but misfortune. Our nervous system isn't just a fiction; it's a part of our physical body, and our soul exists in space, and is inside us, like the teeth in our mouth. It can't be forever violated with impunity. I found it painful to listen to you, Innokentii, when you told us how you were reeducated and became mature in jail. It was like listening to a horse describing how it broke itself in."

WE KNOW VERY LITTLE ABOUT PAIN—and what we don't know makes it hurt all the more. No form of illiteracy in the United States is so widespread or costly as ignorance about pain—what it is, what causes it, how to deal with it without panic. Almost everyone can rattle off the names of at least a dozen drugs that can deaden pain for every conceivable cause—all the way from headaches to hemorrhoids. There is far less knowledge about the fact that ninety percent of pain is self-limiting; that it is not always an indication of poor health; and that, most frequently, it is the result of tension, stress, worry, idleness, boredom, frustration, suppressed rage, insufficient sleep, overeating, a poorly balanced diet, smoking, excessive drinking, inadequate exercise, stale air, or any of the other abuses encountered by the human body in modern society.

AN OFTEN-IGNORED FACT ABOUT PAIN is that the best way to eliminate it is to eliminate the abuse. Instead, many people reach almost instinctively for painkillers. Many doctors are troubled over the extent to which the medical profession today has to deal with ailments or "illnesses" that are well within the capacity of most of us to clear up by ourselves. Doctors' offices are overloaded with people who are mistakenly convinced that something dreadful is about to happen to them, making it difficult for patients genuinely in need of expert diagnosis and treatment to get the attention they need.

MOST MEN THINK THEY ARE IMMORTAL—until they get a cold, when they think they are going to die within the hour.

PAIN IS PART OF THE BODY'S MAGIC. It is the way the body transmits a sign to the brain that something is wrong.

FOR THE PATIENT, illness is not a matter of argument. It is not even a matter of definition. It is a supremely subjective state and is to be taken seriously even when pathology is totally negative. Symptoms that, for the doctor, are verifiably without organic cause are nonetheless real to the patient. These symptoms will not necessarily disappear if the patient is told there is nothing wrong, for the stage is set for progress only when the patient understands why he experiences the symptoms.

THE FACT THAT SYMPTOMS may be psychogenic does not refute the existence of illness any more than it abolishes it. For the patient to understand the difference between functional symptoms and organic causes requires more than an understanding of contrasting definitions. It requires a willingness on the part of the physician to talk things out, to explain that illness often is the result not of germs but of wear and tear, (to use Selye's term for stress) on the mind or body or both. It can be explained, too, that fear, hate, rage, frustration, anxiety, uncertainty, smoking, noise, wretched food, over-eating, over-crowding, and over-working are all involved in wear and tear, especially when they occur in combination. By explicating the connection between those possible causes and the symptoms, and by giving as much weight to the psychogenic factors as to the physiological ones, and then considering possibilities of counter-attack, the physician can help the patient to confront his complaints in a way that may be therapeutic.

DRUGS ARE NOT ALWAYS NECESSARY. Belief in recovery always is.

COMPLICATING THE DOCTOR'S DILEMMA ABOUT DRUGS is the fact that many people tend to regard drugs as though they were automobiles. Each year has to have its new models, and the more powerful the better.

ILLNESS IS NOT A LAUGHING MATTER. Perhaps it ought to be. Laughter is a form of internal jogging. It moves your internal organs around. It enhances respiration. It is an igniter of great expectations.

AN UNDERSTANDING OF THE WAY the placebo works may be one of the most significant developments in medicine in the past century. The placebo does not have imaginary effects though it operates through the imagination. It is quite possible that hope, faith, and the will to live make their registrations on human chemistry the way the placebo does.

NOTHING IS MORE ESSENTIAL, and nothing is more easily resisted, than establishing the extent to which a patient may not fit a diagnosis that has been assigned to him. The dominant strain of an illness may be classifiable, but a vital fraction of exception lies elusively and naggingly within the patient. Every patient, in a very real sense, puts his or her own and unique stamp on a disease.

ONE OF THE BIGGEST NEEDS in medical education today is to attract students who are well-rounded human beings; who will be interested in people and not just in the diseases that affect them; who can comprehend the reality of suffering and not just its symptoms; whose prescription pad will not exclude the human touch and who will take into account not just malevolent microorganisms but all the forces that exercise a downward pull on the health of their patients.

YEARS BEFORE STUDENTS FILE THEIR APPLICATIONS to medical schools, they find themselves pushed in the wrong direction. They tend to become drones rather than fully developed humans. They have little time to find our what the world is about, little time to assess and pursue their other potentialities, most of which would be of value to them in any endeavor involving the healing of human beings. They have time only to prove their academic superiority over their fellows, time only to develop the habits of grade-grabbing that will get them into and through medical school. This will not necessarily make them good doctors.

IT IS TIME TO ASK WHETHER we really want to foster a barracuda psychology for young people who will have to carry the responsibility for maintaining the health and well-being of the American people. Do we really want them clambering over one another, developing their competitive skills ahead of the art of sympathetic understanding? The belief by aspiring doctors that they cannot make it if they are not better scholastically than almost everyone else is hardly likely to start them off in the direction of community medicine or family health care—the main health needs in America today. More likely, a hothouse environment will lead to the continued pursuit of high numbers in different forms—a better address in front of which to hang their shingles, or a specialized practice beyond the means of many of the people who most need their expertise.

GREAT MEDICAL TEACHERS have always impressed upon their students the need to make a careful assessment of everything that may interact in the cause and course of a disease. Hippocrates, the first major historical name in medicine, was both a theoretician and a practitioner. He tried to close existing gaps between the understanding of disease and its treatment. He was quintessentially holistic when he insisted that it is natural for the human body to heal itself and that this process can generally take place even without the intervention of a physician (*vis medicatrix naturae*). He believed that the essential function of the physician—here again Hippocrates was being nothing if not holistic—was to avoid any treatment that might interfere with the healing process or that might do harm (*primum non nocere*). Hippocrates also said it first: "Save the extreme remedies for the extreme diseases." The advice pre-dated antibiotics, anti-hypertensive drugs, tranquilizers, and exotic pain-killers.

A WALL OF SEPARATION has existed for far too long between the public and the physician. The profession of medicine has allowed itself to combine aloofness with authority in a way that tends to produce public resistance or resentment. But an increasing number of physicians have recognized the need for a general demystification of their calling. Similarly, many people who have subscribed to holistic health principles have accepted the fact that their movement is not to be regarded as a total substitute for medical science. There is nothing about the holistic health movement that does not have its sanction in the development of systemic medicine. The auspicious prospect is that the interest of laymen can be knowledgeably sustained in a mutually beneficial and continuing dialogue with the medical profession.

WHATEVER ILLNESS IS OR IS NOT, it is a problem that demands a response. And, just as the physician must train all his or her skills on the degree to which an illness is individualized, so an attack on the illness requires that the physician make a competent estimate of the degree to which the individual's immunological and recuperative capacity can be mobilized in his own behalf. Ultimately, the patient is responsible for his own illness.

The wise physician employs this fact to create not a sense of guilt but a vital sense of participation in treatment and recovery.

THE SCIENCE OF MEDICINE and the art of medicine come together when three things are achieved. The first is the accuracy of the diagnosis. The second is the proportionate nature of the treatment. The third is the full mobilization and release of a patient's healing resources in which robust expectations of full recovery play an important part. If the physician can orchestrate these three elements, he will be doing what he is supposed to do.

THE PHYSICIAN is expected to maintain an open mind about new developments in diagnosis and treatment, but he should not be expected to proceed with treatment in the absence of adequate clinical evidence that it is safe and efficacious. No responsible doctor will experiment on his patients.

THE MOST IMPORTANT THING about science is the scientific method—a way of thinking systematically; a way of assembling evidence and appraising it; a way of conducting experiments so as to predict accurately what will happen under given circumstances; a way of ascertaining and recognizing one's errors; a way of finding the fallacies in long-held ideas. Science itself is constantly changing, largely as the result of the scientific method. The responsible physician should not be expected to depart from this method no matter how great the compulsion or persuasion.

THE GOOD PHYSICIAN is not only a scientist but a philosopher.

THE MOMENT WE ACCEPT the importance of values in the study and practice of medicine, we also accept an obligation to deal with the philosophical issues.

"I FEEL CONVINCED," Claude Bernard, the great medical researcher, wrote more than a century ago, "that there will come a day when physiologists, poets, and philosophers will all speak the same language." That day has not arrived, but at least the sense of a common purpose is beginning to emerge.

PHILOSOPHY SERVES as the great unifier of science and art. Philosophy creates new energies by connecting the human mind to useful questions. Philosophy also provides the means for avoiding collisions not just between past and present but between people who think systematically and people who are accustomed to great leaps of the imagination. Most of all, however, philosophy enables a physician to be governed by attitudes that can supersede and superintend change.

"BRAIN RESEARCH," John C. Eccles said in a symposium on the future of the brain sciences, "is the ultimate problem confronting man ... This is a much bigger problem than cosmology. But for man's brain no problem would exist. The whole drama of the cosmos would be played out before empty stalls."

Neurologists, biologists, biochemists, and psychiatrists may be awed by the mysteries of the human brain, but, fortunately, they do not appear to be intimidated. Dr. Eccles has identified various fields of brain study in which research is necessary: for example, neurogenesis—how new brain cells are formed and grow and how they are converted into a communications network; neuroanatomy—how the central nervous system is connected to the brain and how it operates; neurochemistry—how the brain utilizes exotic and powerful chemicals and how these chemicals carry on vital activity inside the human system; perception—the infinitely complicated process by which neuronal activity is translated into conscious experience.

MANY BRAIN RESEARCHERS AGREE there is probably enough reserve capacity in the brain to meet problems far more demanding and complex than any that have so far confronted the species. The fact that most humans do not use more than fifteen to twenty percent of their available intelligence would seem to indicate that the principle need of humanity is not for a better brain but for some way to make better use of the brains we have.

The concept of reserve brainpower waiting to be unlocked is comforting at a time when philosophers are asking whether the human race is smart enough to survive. The conditions of life have been running down. The dominant intelligence, however, has been trained on tribal business rather than on the operation of human society as a whole. It is possible that this challenge is related to the need for a new consciousness. It is a consciousness that can take into account the condition of the species rather than the condition of any of its subdivisions.

DOES NOTHING HAPPEN inside a physician's mind when he reads that governments are preparing to turn loose on humans more disease organisms in one day than have ravaged humans in all the years since the early Egyptians discovered the connection between impure water and raging fever? Should a physician who has invested most of his life in an effort to combat illness have no particular response or responsibility to keep the government itself from becoming a manufacturer of epidemics?

ETHICAL QUESTIONS EXIST on concentric rings. Any break, especially in the outer ring, produces breakdowns on the inner rings as well. By the outer ring, I have in mind the management of society. An illustration of a breakdown in human values in the management of society is the decision by government to manufacture nerve gases and to breed and stockpile virulently toxigenic bacteria as weapons of war. Not even war relieves us of the obligation to make a distinction between essential ingenuity in a fight for survival and the extraneous exercise of random and unlimited malevolence.

CONSIDER THE QUESTION of moral integrity inherent in a situation in which the government appropriates large sums of money to subsidize those who grow tobacco but at the same time warns its citizens that tobacco can cause cancer. The moral fiasco is compounded when the government subsidizes the glamorization of tobacco for sale abroad. Can the medical profession regard such actions casually? Does the profession have no function except to wait for the casualties to be trundled in? If so, how do physicians differentiate themselves from morticians, whose calling confines them to situations beyond recall or redemption? If physicians are to regard themselves as a vital part of the life-sustaining process and not as mechanical attendants on an assembly belt of human breakdown, can they avoid moral decisions with implications for the health of the total community?

TO PRACTICE MEDICINE at a time when the earth has become a single geographic community calls for an enlargement of the Hippocratic Oath. In today's world the physician must make his commitment not just to individual life but to the institution of life. To the extent that medical societies are concerned only with professional questions, they restrain physicians from involvement in ethical issues. Insulated in that manner from his central role, the physician can trail happily after illness while ignoring his obligation to help humanize society and to make it safe and fit for human beings.

SURELY THE MEDICAL PROFESSION should have more than a bandaging role in any confrontation with violence in American life. It need not wait until casual attitudes toward brutality are translated into court cases. Even the articulation of a position on the subject can serve as a rallying point. A useful precedent is the American Medical Association's stand on television violence.

THE ENTERTAINMENT MEDIA have the notion that people do not consider themselves entertained unless they see humans kicked around and made to spurt blood in color. People who have been conditioned by mindless violence and mayhem can hardly be expected to form a cheering section for the development of health care programs to relieve human suffering.

TRUTH TELLING TO PATIENTS is often debated as though the only issue is whether physicians are obligated to tell what they know. Far more consequential are these issues:

Does the physician always know the truth?

Is there an art to truth-telling as there is to everything else?

What is the effect of truth on the patient? To what extent can total candor undermine the physician's effectiveness in dealing with the ravages of disease? How does unvarnished disclosure affect the quality of life—and therefore the quality of dying?

Is the fear of malpractice suits causing some physicians—understandably, perhaps—to be explicit to the point of overkill?

These questions are not merely rhetorical exercises. They

affect medical practice today in fundamental ways. They deserve to be probed.

WALTER CANNON, one of the great figures of American medicine in the twentieth century, once wrote a paper about the hex of the voodoo doctor and why it was that people died on cue. What Dr. Cannon concluded was that it was not the hex that killed people but their own acceptance of the certainty they were going to die. The will to die replaced the will to live. If people can keep an appointment with death, they can keep an appointment with life. If they can be programmed to die, they can be programmed to live. The physician's job is to program human beings to live.

THE BEST PHYSICIANS are not just superb diagnosticians but men who understand the phenomenal energy (and therefore curative propensity) that flows out of an individual's capacity to retain an optimistic belief and attitude toward problems and human affairs in general. It is a perversion of rationalism to argue that words like "hope" or "faith" or "love" or "grace" are without physiological significance. The benevolent emotions are necessary not just because they are pleasant but because they are regenerative. The will to live produces a responsive chemistry.

HANS SELYE has been primarily concerned with the *overworked* or exhausted adrenal glands. But what about the effects of the *underworked* adrenal glands? Adrenal insufficiency, whether from depletion or atrophy, is the problem. Are we to assume there are no hazards in inaction and purposelessness? Does the body pay no price for emotional, mental, and physical lethargy and stupefaction?

I CAN IMAGINE no greater satisfaction for a person, in looking back on his life and work, than to have been able to give some people, however few, a feeling of genuine pride in belonging to the human species and, beyond that, a zestful yen to justify that pride.